2024 NEW EDITION

PLUMBING BIBLE

THE ULTIMATE DIY GUIDE TO SOLVE ANY LEAKS, CLOGS, AND PLUMBING WOES WITH CONFIDENCE AND COST-FREE. STEP-BY-STEP INSTRUCTIONS AND MONEY-SAVING STRATEGIES FOR HOMEOWNERS

10 IN 1

CONNOR BENNETT

PLUMBING BIBLE 10 In 1

The Ultimate DIY Guide to Solve any Leaks, Clogs, and Plumbing Woes with Confidence and Cost-Free. Step-by-Step Instructions and Money-Saving Strategies for Homeowners

First Edition August 2023

PLUMBING BIBLE

[10 In 1]

The Ultimate DIY Guide to Solve any Leaks, Clogs, and Plumbing Woes with Confidence and Cost-Free. Step-by-Step Instructions and Money-Saving Strategies for Homeowners

CONNOR BENNETT

TABLE OF CONTENTS

INTRODUCTION

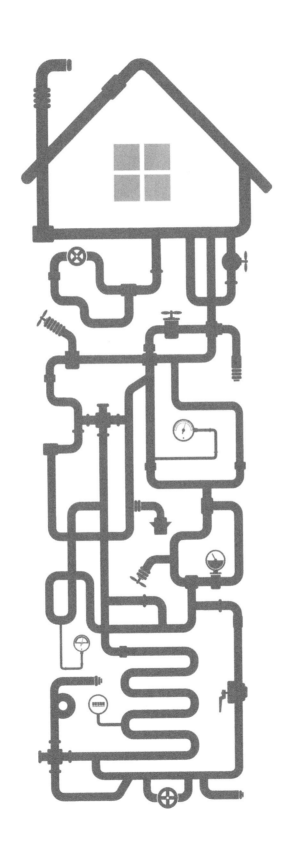

Due to the advantages, every home needs a reliable plumbing system. Its importance also lies in the fact that it improves our quality of life. The plumbing system makes the public's access to water for health, hygiene, and well-being possible. Easy access to clean and potable water is possible with a good plumbing system. We often take this facility for granted. The quantity of water utilized by plumbing fixtures, such as faucets, showerheads, and toilets, has significantly decreased because of innovative plumbing technologies. Water sustainability requires increased plumbing efficiency. Commercial facilities can save even more money by installing a high-efficiency plumbing system. Plumbing also makes homes and lifestyles beautiful and comfortable. A solid plumbing layout can help stop pipes from leaking. Imagine waking up to water pools and leaking pipes at home. These issues are not only uncomfortable, but they also make one feel uneasy. Additionally, we need a considerable amount of time to manage problems related to pipe leaks and clogged drains. To fix plumbing problems correctly, you must either hire a plumber or have a solid understanding of plumbing. You can successfully clean drains, dispose of garbage, and manage sinks, fixtures as well as faucets. It will be easy for you to identify and fix leaks, unclog toilets, clean main lines, fix busted pipes, repair sewer lines, clean storm drains, etc., by learning about plumbing systems and how to oversee plumbing issues. Plumbing difficulties can cause significant complications and health dangers. By keeping the plumbing system maintained regularly and taking care of plumbing problems when they arise, you may avoid all of these problems. This book will assist you in learning more about the plumbing system, its components, and procedures and tactics for resolving plumbing problems as they arise without having to hire a professional plumber. By following the step-by-step directions, using useful guidance, and using troubleshooting tips, you will also discover the proper methods for managing and safely resolving plumbing issues. You'll feel more capable of handling plumbing issues and experience less dread and worry when confronted with unforeseen circumstances. On top of that, this book will not only help you in saving money but also in improving your quality of life by enjoying a comfortable home environment in an economical way.

CHAPTER 1
INTRODUCTION TO HOUSEHOLD PLUMBING

Plumbing is a skill that enables you to set up, maintain, and update the piping, fixtures, and appliances in your home. If you have adequate knowledge of plumbing, addressing problems with storm drainage systems is certainly possible. There should be a reliable potable water supply system in your home. Additionally, the home needs to have a reliable drainage system. You should have sufficient fixtures, tools, and equipment on hand to address and resolve plumbing concerns. You must take action to ensure that your home has an adequate amount of potable water, a correctly installed drainage system, and no problems that could cause water to become contaminated.

1.1 HOUSEHOLD PLUMBING SYSTEM

Pressure, along with gravity and maintaining water level, are the fundamental principles of plumbing. With this knowledge, you may unravel its "mysteries" and prevent dozens of issues related to plumbing in the home. The plumbing system of the home consists of two subsystems. One subsystem introduces freshwater, and one subsystem helps in removing the wastewater. The home's water is subject to pressure at the point of its entry. It moves into your house with substantial force. This makes it easy for it to move to various locations of the home, both upstairs and downstairs. Water entering your home flows through a meter, which is the amount of water used by you and your family. Normally, the valve for shutting off the main water is located close to the meter. Otherwise, the home could quickly become flooded in the event of a bursting pipe. Conversely, you might not want to shut off your whole water supply in case the leakage problem is restricted to a toilet, shower, or basin. It is advised that all fittings have specific valves for stopping the water. The main supply is meant to address your needs for water that is both cold and in the required volume. However, there is still a step needed for the hot water supply. The water heater and the system for cold water are connected by only one pipe. By turning off and on the heating elements of the heater, as needed, a thermostat helps you to maintain the desired temperature. The typical setting for a water heater for homes lies in the range of 140-160 degrees F; however, 120 F is quite enough. Moreover, this setting is also more economical. You should know that automatic dishwashers can work effectively at higher temperatures as the hot water cleans the dishes properly. However, there are built-in water heaters in dishwashers that can increase the water's temperature by another 20 degrees F.

The internal systems of the home are the same whether linked with a sewer or septic system. Supply systems rely on pressure, while systems meant for drainage do not depend on pressure. On the contrary, the removal of trash and other waste from the home is possible due to the drainage pipes' downward pitches or angles in the direction of the sewage system. The trash is emptied with the aid of gravity. The sewage line aids in keeping the waste moving to a tank for septic waste facilities. The system has more to it than it first appears, including clean outs, traps, and vents. The home's roof has vents that stick out, which let air into the drainpipes. Wastewater couldn't properly drain through the vents lacking a constant availability of air. As a result, the traps' water must be discharged. The drainage system's essential components are traps. There is a trap for each sink. This trap is visible. A seal is formed in the trap after enough water has been allowed to remain there to prevent sewer gas from coming up into your home. Basin water rushes with sufficient power with the help of the trap. Then it moves out through the drainpipe. There must be a trap on every fixture. Toilets are self-trapped. Therefore, a drain does not need a separate trap. Older bathtubs usually include drum traps that serve as a seal against sewer gas as well as a collection point for hair and debris. Thus they prevent the drains from clogging. However, drum traps do not meet the general standards and requirements. Kitchen faucets often have grease collectors designed specifically to prevent clogging from grease. Grease, as well as hair, are frequently the factors that block the drain. Therefore, there are clean-out plugs in traps that help facilitate the removal or dissolving of any blockage. The system for drainage is called DWV, as it includes all of these parts. All DWV components need to be present as well as in good operational condition so that they can make it easy for water to pass easily and waste to go out appropriately. To further comprehend the system, look at the basement pipes of the house.

The subsystems of Service and Irrigation

Both the part of the system responsible for supplying and the component for disposal are considered to be separate processes because there is no connection amongst them. But certain distinctions do exist between these systems, and it is because of these differences that your overall water system is useful. Any link in the drainage as well as supply systems is known as a fixture in the field of plumbing. Fixtures include bathtubs, sinks, and toilets. An outside faucet and washing machine are additional instances of fixtures. furnishings, specialized mechanisms that assist in collecting and dumping wastewater, keep the wastewater disposal while providing streams distinct from one another. Fixtures are also known as fittings. When repairing certain fixtures, you won't have to close the primary shutoff valve because those fixtures come equipped with their own autonomous supply shutdown valves. Make sure that every family member is aware of where the main valve for stopping water is located and how to operate it. Label the central shutdown valve so that you know exactly where to look for it. Before doing any work on the drainage system, turning off the primary source of water is a necessary and strongly encouraged step. Before installing or changing pipes in your home, make sure that you check with the official in charge of the plumbing code in your area. You'll discover what is allowed. You will also know the tasks which are not permissible. If you can fix plumbing issues at your home yourself, then you can save enough money.

1.2 IMPORTANCE OF BASIC KNOWLEDGE OF HOUSEHOLD PLUMBING

Planning a household or commercial building requires careful consideration of plumbing. Your pipes frequently have a backup to blame for this. This issue may pose serious issues and health hazards. A well-designed sewerage system will partition the garbage and clean

water supply lines via air gaps, physical barriers, and code compliance. If you have the plumbing in your property serviced regularly, you can reduce the risk of water pollution in the house you live in. Poor sanitation can lead to a wide range of issues and even catastrophes. One such instance is spills. Wall collapse and mold development are only two of the additional severe problems that might occur from ignoring the source of the leak. Over time, a plumbing system's leak may turn into a serious problem. Pipes that are hidden inside the exterior surfaces of a building frequently make it possible for tiny leaks to be undiscovered until something catastrophic takes place, resulting in considerable damage. Eventually, having a drainage system that is regularly serviced and cared for could end up saving you money. Leaks in the sewage may entail wasting funds on repairs to the structure of the home in addition to all the fixings to the plumbing that need to be done. If you decide to invest in dependable plumbing components and keep up with the scheduled upkeep on them, you stand a good chance of saving a significant amount of dough in the future. The optimum circumstances for mold development are created when there are breaches in the drinking water supplies. If mold is allowed to develop unnoticed in the home, it can lead to a variety of health issues, including difficulty with breathing, and it can also cause structural damage.

 ## 1.3 TOP REASONS FOR ACQUIRING BASIC KNOWLEDGE OF HOUSEHOLD PLUMBING

Plumbing helps to make lifestyles and homes more beautiful and enjoyable. Kitchens and bathrooms not only help in addressing basic needs but also offer places where we can enjoy our food, take baths, and spend leisure time with our family members. Some people, however, have good skills. Consequently, they enjoy being able to complete tasks around the house. Actually, DIY abilities are gradually declining, especially among younger individuals. Even while you can always rely on professionals to do your tasks, everyone should at least have a basic understanding of plumbing. These straightforward tips could save you some money, but they could also come in handy should you need to act swiftly in an emergency.

You can save the property from getting damaged if you know the location of the stop tap.

The stop tap should be used to turn off the water as soon as a leak is discovered. You could afford to spend 20 minutes searching the house for a slow leak, but you can't really afford to do that if there is a flood. Because of this, knowing its location is crucial before a problem arises. Make sure it is reachable as well as you can turn it when you find it. Know the location and importance of condensate pipe.

The main function of condensate pipes is to help in expelling moisture from the boiler. It is typically situated on the exterior of the premises. The possibility exists that the condenser pipe will freeze due to the freezing temperatures. As a direct consequence of this, the furnace will no longer operate properly. Naturally, this is the time of year when you most need the heating and hot water, but fixing the problem is actually fairly straightforward. You should go out and check if your boiler is working in temperatures below zero. A frozen pipe can be defrosted by either using warm water or hot water. The boiler should thereafter be able to restart. Although you may simply solve the problem yourself, many people would seek a gas professional to complete this operation since they think their boiler is broken.

What should be done to address drainage issues?

Don't ignore the problem and wait for it to go away if water is draining from sinks, bathtubs, or showers more slowly. Before you have to hire a plumber, you might be able to fix it or, at the very least, rule things out. There is typically a blockage someplace, which is the main problem. You can attempt to clear it by using a caustic substance, such as soda bicarbonate. You can also use a product for unclogging the drain or vinegar solution if it's merely trash, such as food in kitchen sinks and hair/soap/etc..

Acting fast can make all the difference in a heating or plumbing emergency, whether it's to reduce costs or even save your life. Knowing your alternatives beforehand can enable you to respond quickly when the moment comes, rather than just assuming you will know what to do. We'd advise making sure everyone in your house is aware of what to do:

- If a leak or flood occurs
- If the alarm for carbon monoxide turns off or you smell gas
- Know when to DIY in case of a boiler emergency.

1.4 MAJOR PLUMBING PROBLEMS IN THE HOME AND HOW TO ADDRESS THEM

When you have a home, then you should be ready to handle issues related to plumbing. You should know that outdated fixtures create certain problems. Moreover, wear and tear can also cause certain issues. The way you are maintaining and using specific systems could also result in certain issues. Listed below are the typical problems you might have, along with information on why they occur and what can be done to address them.

Dripping Faucets

Dripping faucets are inconvenient, expensive, and wasteful. screw that has become worn out could sometimes be the cause for such dripping. Fortunately, both of these components are simple to replace when they become worn. At other moments, the dripping sound could be caused by corrosion or an incorrect setup of the faucet. You need to clean the valve seat on a scheduled basis if you want to prevent corrosion.

Leaky Pipes

Numerous issues, such as obstinate blockages, improperly laid out pipes, damage in joints of pipes, broken seals, or damaged pipes, and high water pressure, can result in leaky pipes if a pipe is leaking. You should drain the water supply. Locate the water main shut-off valve, which is typically found in the garage, basement, or crawl space. After that, flush each toilet of the house, as well as turn on all of your faucets to release any water or pressure that may still be in the water line. The damaged pipe should stop leaking once you've completed this. The epoxy putty can be applied to the broken pipe for another quick and simple plumbing leak fix. The epoxy putty can fix any tiny leak in a pipe after being applied, hardening it into a solid surface.

Running toilets

A toilet that has started to malfunction can result in the wastage of a significant amount of water. Most frequently, issues with the refill tube, old flapper seals or flush valves, and improperly sized flapper chains are to blame for running toilets.

The water pressure is low

The lack of water pressure is sometimes an indication of additional plumbing concerns, such as pipeline deterioration, hidden water damage throughout your residence, or blockage in the sewage or draining. You need to arrange the setting of the valve that is used to reduce pressure. It is normally located in your home near your water meter. If the reading on your pressure gauge is low, make a few minor changes to your regulator.

Clogged or Slow Drains

If there is only one drain in your home that is clogged, the issue is localized to just that one area.. One of the prime reasons for these blockages in drains is the accumulation of soap, hair as well as other materials over time. Regular drain cleaning may be the best approach to resolving this problem.

Failure of the Sump pump

A sump pump can start to malfunction for a number of reasons. Their malfunctioning is typically caused by a number of factors, such as an excessive amount of water, such as after a severe downpour, clogged discharge pipes, poor installation of sump pumps, and outdated sump pumps. Your sump pump may have ceased working due to an old or damaged float. Starting a sump pump should not pose any problem if the sump pit is filled with water. You might have to replace the float in case you fail to start a sump pump.

Issues with the water heater

Typically, difficulties with heating elements, silt buildup in plumbing, faulty electrical connections, and inappropriate water heater installation are what lead to water heater problems. If you fail to get hot water from the water heater in your home, check to see whether the circuit breaker or a fuse has tripped. If that isn't the problem, then the heating element could need to be changed if it has burned out.

1.5 ESSENTIAL TOOLS AND EQUIPMENT FOR PLUMBING REPAIRS

Give below is the list, along with the use of the best plumbing tools that you must have to fix plumbing issues on your own.

Plumbing Hand Tools

Wrenches

Given below is the list and description of wrenches.

Basin wrench

Handy for faucets.

Faucet key

Used for opening and closing faucets and sillcocks.

Tools for Pipe Work

Tubing cutters and plastic pipe cutters

Used for removing, replacing, and resizing copper or plastic piping.

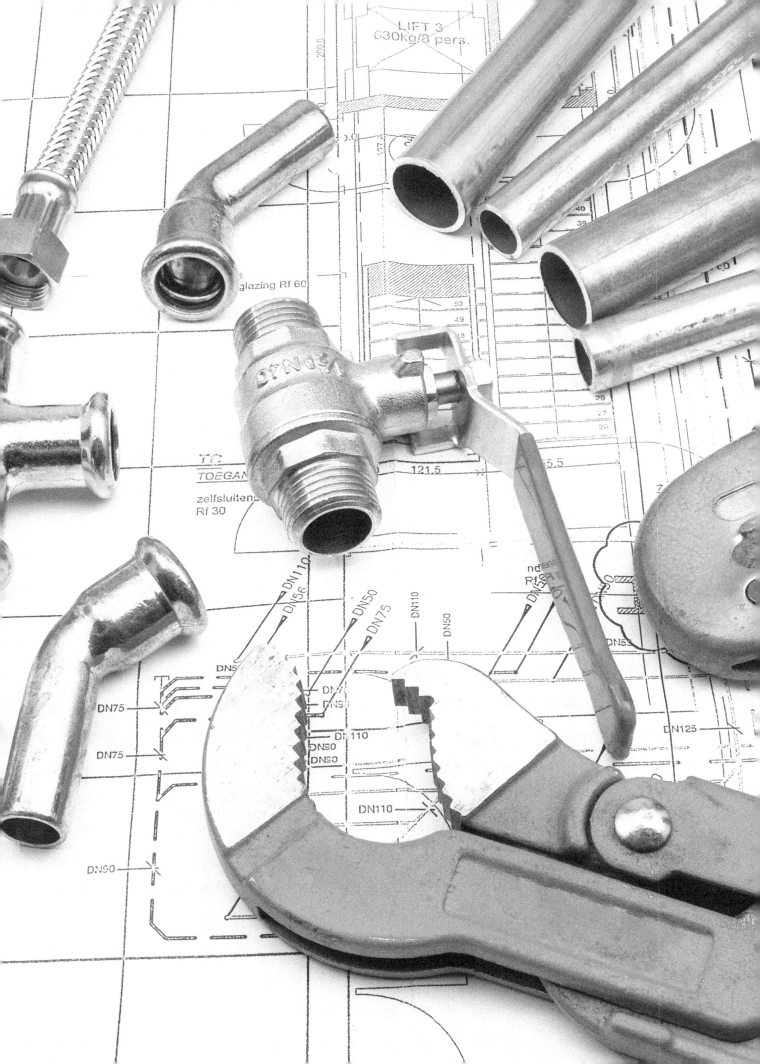

Plumber's torch

Use it to solder and seal new pipes.

Thread sealing tape

Prevent threaded joint connections from leaking by using this tape.

Pliers

Used for loosening and tightening smaller nuts and bolts.

Press fitting systems

Helps to connect pipes securely.

Tools for Clearing Clogs and Blockages

Plungers

Assists in producing significantly more suction as compared to a consumer plunger.

Hand Auger

Helps in clearing clogs.

Snake Machine

Helps in clearing deep clogs.

Inspection camera

Inspect the extent of clogging by using an inspection camera.

Safety Tools

Goggles

Goggles are necessary for examining and soldering leaks.

Gloves

For safe hands and to perform your job easily, you must wear gloves.

Heat shields/pads

Protects you from heat and fire.

PEX pipe expander & fittings

This looks like an instrument for drilling and is used to widen a pipe's oral tradition, allowing an aluminum component to be installed.

Crimpers

By stretching or deforming one or both metal pieces, these aid in joining several pieces of metal or other material.

Stubby screwdriver

Utilized to tighten or loosen a screw in an awkward location.

Flow rate calculator

Based on diameter and velocity, it will assist you in swiftly calculating the speed of water running in a pipe.

Pipe volume calculator

Useful for calculating the water volume a piping segment can carry and for calculating the weight of the water inside those pipes.

 # 1.6 SAFETY IN HOME PLUMBING WORK

Listed below are the safety tips for doing plumbing work at home.

Knowledge is essential

Check all relevant local construction and plumbing codes to determine what tasks can be completed without professional help and what tasks can be completed by yourself.

Close the water supply

Turn off the water to be safe if there's a slight likelihood that the task at hand can include dealing with the water supply.

Ensure protective measures for the Eyes

To do the task, plumbers require eye protection. Put on safety glasses that won't fog and keep them on.

Ensure protective measures for the Ears

A plumbing workplace is full of loud, penetrating noises. If ears are not protected, these noises damage a plumber's hearing over time.

Hands and arms must be covered

Burrs and other potential cut dangers are avoided with long sleeves. Gloves are disliked by certain professionals, although they are crucial in the fight against infection. As a result, they continue to be essential pieces of safety gear whenever you have to deal with mold, toxic industrial chemicals, or garbage.

Feet need to be protected

Boots that are slip-resistant shield the entire body from falls. They also protect your feet. Even some boots are resistant to a variety of waste materials.

Take care of your lungs

A plumber's lungs are shielded from mold and harmful toxins by masks.

Remember to exercise caution

Combustibles, electricity, and water do not combine. It's time to leave if gas is smelled. You need to identify the cause.

Tools must be used with caution.

While using power tools, use caution and adhere to the manufacturer's instructions.

Do not cut blindly

You must not cut or drill into anything unless you are aware of what is concealed beneath the surface.

Whenever handling any tool or chemically based, make sure to familiarize yourself with the packaging and instructions.

Check the labels on items and equipment for warnings and be prepared for emergencies.

Employ the Proper Tools

Without mentioning the proper tools, our plumbing safety advice would fall short. The correct instruments facilitate a quicker, safer, and easier task. Preparation includes planning on potential tool requirements.

 ## 1.7 GLOSSARY OF PLUMBING TERMS

You cannot do your DIY work unless you are aware of the plumbing terms and terminology. The undermentioned plumbing glossary will help you address plumbing issues immediately.

Access panel

It is a hole next to a fixture in the ceiling. You can repair electrical or plumbing systems with it.

Angle stop

Water flow is stopped while the connected item is being repaired using this device.

Anode rod

You can find the anode rod inside the water heater.

Backwater valve

A backwater valve stops the sewage from coming back in.

Ball check valve

It is installed on a water pipe to control the direction of water flow.

Ballcock

The water flow is managed by the ballcock in the toilet tank, which is operated by gravity.

Branch

Any auxiliary component of the drainage system is a branch.

Branch vent

Vents are connected with a vent stack by a branch vent.

Check valve

It is mounted on a pipe to enable one-way water flow.

Cleanout plug

It is located in a drainpipe or trap. The cleanout plug provides accessibility to the drain line so that any obstruction in the pipes can be removed.

Closet auger

A flexible rod called a closet auger is utilized to access the toilet's trap and clear any obstructions.

Closet bend

The toilet's drain is joined to the closet flange via the closet bend.

Closet flange

The term "closet flanges" refers to the circle that sits on the ground underneath and holds the closet bending in place.

Diaphragm

It is a permeable membrane that aids in controlling water flow and accumulation inside a valve.

Dip tube

The water heater tank's bottom receives cold water from the dip tube.

Drip leg

A pipe put at the lowest section of a gas line is known as the drip leg. Condensation and debris are collected in the capped-off area.

Escutcheon

It is a protective covering that covers the fixture hole underneath the faucet handle.

Fall/Flow

The slope required to ensure adequate water flow in pipes is referred to as the fall.

Fixture

The plumbing component that carries water and/or waste is referred to as a fixture.

Flapper

The water tank, as well as the toilet bowl, are connected by the flapper valve.

Float ball

The plastic ball fastened to the ballcock is known as the float ball. The position of the float ball affects how much water rises and falls in the tank.

Floor flange

A toilet is connected to the sewage line by the floor flange.

Gas cock

A main gas line's gas cock makes it possible to turn off the gas.

A toilet that operates by gravity

A gravity-operated toilet works by water's downward pressure in the tank.

Gray water

The fluid waste that originates from typical fixtures—but not toilets—is referred to as gray water.

Horizontal branch

The horizontal branch connects waste stacks to plumbing fixtures.

Horizontal run

The distance that liquid covers between a pipe's entry and exit points.

Hose bib

It is a type of faucet.

Main line

The main line carries water from the street-level water company meter to the branch pipes that are located all around your house.

Nipple

Short pipes called nipples are used to join couplings as well as additional fittings.

Pressure-reducing valve or PRV

To maintain a consistent water pressure for domestic consumption, the PRV limits the amount of water that may be accessed from the water companies' supply.

PVC

PVC pipes are resilient plastic pipes used in vent, waste, and drainage systems.

Rim holes

The toilet bowl's rim has a number of tiny holes in it.

Saddle valve

For swift connections between low-demand devices, utilize the saddle valve.

Septic system

A small sewage treatment system called a septic tank is used in households without a connection to public sewage systems.

Straight stop valve

When performing repairs, this valve is utilized to shut off the water supply.

Sump pump

In often flooded basements, a sump pump is employed.

Supply line

A conduit composed of steel or plastic that extends through the primary sewer line to a fitting in the bathroom and then returning to the central connection anew is called a source connection.

T&P valve

A water tank's excess heat or pressure can be safely released using the temperature and pressure relief valve.

Tailpiece

The pipe that connects a fixture and a trap is the tailpiece.

Trap

It helps to prevent sewer odor from entering the home.

Trapway

The waste outlet and the toilet bowl are connected via a trapway.

Trip lever

The flush handle, as well as actuating arm of a toilet tank, are located on the trip lever. The toilet flushes as a result of the trip lever's attachment to the flapper.

Vent stack

Outside the house, the vent stack produces gas and odors.

Water hammer

When pipes are turned on or off, they make a loud noise as well as a vibration known as a "water hammer." The rapid rush or pause in the pipes' water causes the water to hammer.

CHAPTER 2
REPAIRING WATER LEAKS

The majority of homeowners ought to be able to locate and correctly fix water leaks. Depending on the sort of leak and your degree of competence, fixing a leaky pipe, a broken fixture, or a toilet that's running is frequently a simple fix. Leaking pipes can severely damage floors as well as ceilings and produce mold inside the drywall of the home if they are not fixed right away.

 ## 2.1 IDENTIFYING AND LOCATING WATER LEAKS

Listed below are ways for identifying and locating water leaks.

Water Meter Test

This test can be conducted to find water leaks that are hidden. If you discover that readings are changing, then you should be prepared to fix the leakage issue.

Look for signs of running water

In the absence of any apparent leakage issues, one may listen for running water. Sometimes you can hear a water leaking sound. This sound can come from walls or floors.

Check all of the appliances in the home to see if any of them are leaking

Before you can determine which machine has a leak, you need to disconnect all of the equipment in order to search for water to circulate from equipment.

Check your toilet for any signs of leaking

Put a few tablespoons of food coloring into the water container, then wait until daylight to check for any problems in the bathroom. If you notice still color in the bowl of the bathroom the next morning despite your having flushed it, there is an obstruction in the toilet. Utility bills can also give a clue.

At times, the water bill will provide you with signs about leaks you are not aware of. There will be water leaking from any source if you discover an unexpected or significant spike in your consumption of water.

Check if the Walls are wet

There is a definite leakage issue if the family members see wetness in the laundry room, kitchen, or bathroom.

 ## 2.2 REPAIRING DAMAGED OR CRACKED PIPES

You should follow the steps mentioned below to repair damaged pipes.

There are shut-off valves on the underside of the toilet as well as under the sinks in your kitchen and bathroom. You might occasionally need to shut off your main water valve, which is outside your property. Then, before starting the water leak repair, the faucets should be run to clear the pipes.

Ensure there is not water in the pipes and that they are totally dry

Ensure that any water that has gathered on nearby surfaces has been cleaned up. This will allow you to apply the putty to a dry surface.

Silicone tape should be used for fixing leaks

Cut a piece that is 6-8 inches (15-20 cm) or longer and press it against the hole's side. Then it should be wrapped over the hole multiple times whilst pulling it taut. To secure it, encircle it once more with tape, but this time avoid stretching the tape.

Plumbing Putty can be applied to fix pipe leakage

It is an effective repair material. You can use it to patch as well as fix broken pipes. To begin, take a bit of the epoxy putty out of the container and mix it to activate it. When the pipe repair epoxy acquires an ivory-colored hue, it is appropriate to be applied to the leakage.. Make a layer of putty that is five inches thick, then completely cover the leak with the putty. To make a watertight seal, press hard around the putty's edges.

Water Leak can be repaired by using clumps

Rubber gaskets are attached to the ends of pipe clamps to provide a watertight seal around the damaged pipe and prevent leaks.

Think about replacing the Leaky Pipe

You must replace the damaged portion of the pipe if you want a more long-lasting fix. You must get the proper-sized fixtures, couplings, and pipes. If you don't currently possess these things, you will need to go out and get them before continuing.

 ## 2.3 HOW TO REPLACE FAULTY SEALS AND VALVES?

Grit and mineral deposits can clog main water shut-off valves. They also result in slow leaks. To complete the substitution, and you will require a number of instruments, substances, and supplies:

- Adjustable wrench
- Three-fourths-inch ball valve
- Pipe wrench
- Plumbers tape
- 4-in-1 screwdriver
- Leather washers

First Step-Clogged Valve

Check the "street-side" valve near the house's water connection point. Check that valve, which is also old, to ensure that it completely closes and then reopens. Mineral deposits and minute grit particles can slowly accumulate in an old valve and prevent the valve from closing all the way. In the unlikely scenario that the primary shutoff valve located at the sidewalk needs to be changed, you should contact your local water service company.

Second step -The old valve should be loosened

Examine the "bonding jumper" that connects the clamp with the meter's house side with the street side's clamp. The old valve's nipple can then be removed easily. You must undo the connection on the water meter's "house side" in order to take out the old valve. Typically, there is a washer for sealing. It is made up of leather.

Third step -The new valve should be installed

Most likely, there is a pipe attached to the valve that is leaking. Purchase a replacement threaded ball valve. The new nipple has to be installed along with the purchased ball valve. The leather washer also needs to be replaced. The water should be turned on. The coupling nut should be tightened.

Fourth step- Washers

Leather washers should be used as they do not crack or dry out.

2.4 HOW TO FIX DRIPPING FAUCETS?

There are four types of faucets.

* Frisbee Valves
* Fittings that Use Compression Washers
* Ball Fixtures
* Fittings that use cartridges

DIY repairs to a dripping faucet can result in significant cost savings. If you want to fix running fixtures such as faucets take the instructions that are stated below.

First Step- Water should be turned off

You can find the fixture shut-off valves beneath the sink, then turn the handles in a clockwise direction to turn off the water. If your faucet isn't equipped with any shutoff valves, stop the house's main water supply.

Second Step - Faucet Handles should be disassembled

It is possible to take the levers away of a leaking faucet in a variety of distinctive methods, determined by the kind of fixtures you have. For common fixtures, you can expose the handle screws by removing the handle's top cap with a flathead screwdriver. Then the handles should be pulled off after unscrewing.

Third Step - The valve Stem should be detached

You can view the inner valve stem or cartridge once the faucet handle has been removed. Additionally, this must be taken out. Brass valve stems on compression faucets can be unscrewed. Cartridge faucets are easily removed. You can consult your faucet's guide or find instructions online if you need help.

Fourth Step – Sink parts should be inspected

After all parts have been taken out, they need to be inspected carefully to confirm the steps that need to be taken for the replacement or fixing of a leaking faucet.

Fifth Step - Damaged Parts should be replaced

Replace any worn-out, broken, or outdated components. The parts you require can be found at your neighborhood hardware shop. Bringing the old components into a hardware shop and asking for exact copies is the best and simplest approach to getting the appropriate parts for your leaky faucet.

Sixth Step – Valves should be sanitized

Once the stem or cartridge has been eliminated, monitor the body of the valve. There is typically mineral accumulation. White vinegar should be poured over the valve seat. Then it should be allowed to sit there for a few minutes to clean it. Once removed, scrub the sink's other components to bring back its smoothness and shine.

Seventh Step - The faucet should be installed

After replacing the parts and cleaning everything, the faucet should be reassembled.

 ## 2.5 WATER PRESSURE CHANGES: REMEDIES

Listed below are the steps that can be taken for identifying and improving water pressure in the home.

It is important to keep an eye out for leakage

When pipes have been harmed, it is more difficult for rainwater to flow through them. The most straightforward method for determining the extent to which faulty infrastructure is impeding the flow of moisture in your place of residence is to look for leaking. Check any visible pipes for moisture and indications of rust or accumulation. Pipe replacements provide more than only raise water pressure, despite the fact that it could be a costly replacement. Additionally, it will lessen the possibility of additional leaks and the danger of drinking water that is not safe.

Clogs should be checked

Hard water mineral deposits can accumulate over time and decrease water pressure. Although clogs can form anywhere in the pipeline, they are most commonly found and fixed by homeowners in shower-heads as well as sink faucets. Do what is required to clean the shower-head. The faucet aerator or water restrictor on a sink faucet or kitchen sprayer is nothing more than a fine mesh filter that distributes the water flow. Over time, mineral deposits may cause the mesh to accumulate. To increase water flow, you can quickly clean the filter by finding it just inside the spout & unscrewing the faucet's end.

The valve for reducing water should be adjusted

Adjusting the pressure-reducing valve, which is normally located in your home near your water meter, is a quick and simple approach to boosting water pressure. Start by making minor adjustments to the water pressure, and then keep testing to see if it gets better inside your house.

A Water Pressure Booster can be installed

Hire a qualified plumber to install a water-pressure booster pump if the flow in the municipal or well water is the issue. These strong electric pumps are designed to increase incoming pressure to the appropriate level.

2.6 IDENTIFYING AND LOCATING WATER LEAKS IN THE GARDEN IRRIGATION SYSTEM

Your lawn irrigation system may be leaking if you see water accumulated on your landscaping following or in between watering cycles. An inadequate lawn irrigation system can waste water, require expensive repairs and replacements, and destroy your landscape. Listed below are the common causes of a leaking lawn irrigation system.

Broken Sprinkler Heads

Leakage in a drip system for the grass is typically caused by one of several factors, with the most common of which involves faulty head connections. Water shoots out of cracked, fractured, or damaged sprinkler heads, and water pools around the affected sprinkler head location, make them often simple to spot. There are several things that may damage a sprinkler head, including lawnmowers, vehicles, aging, wear, and tear, or even someone accidentally treading on it. In order for your irrigation system to function properly, any sprinkler heads that are broken need to be replaced immediately.

Valve Leaks

Your sprinkler system's valves may degrade and succumb to normal wear and tear over time, which can cause valve leaks. Valve leaks are simple to identify since they begin as a slow, constant drip that continues even when the system is turned off. This allows water to keep coming out of a sprinkler. An obstruction in the valve's mechanism, which may be a sign of low-head drainage or that the valve needs to be replaced, is the usual cause of leaky valves.

Line Breaks

The mainlines, as well as lateral lines—two water pipelines that can get damaged—commonly make up irrigation systems. Consequently, one of the first steps in repairing a broken water line is to identify whether the break is in the mainline or a lateral line. Water will typically collect on your lawn and the surrounding areas when there is a mainline break; thus, the system needs to be turned off entirely at once. The lateral line leak is a little harder to find, but you usually only notice pooling after your system is turned off. The irrigation system may continue to operate even if there is a fault in the lateral line by simply shutting off the zone where the break is located until your system can be fixed. Water lines can be damaged by environmental elements like tree roots, normal wear and tear, ground movement, or unintentional actions like digging in your yard.

2.7 REPAIRING WATER LEAKS IN THE GARDEN IRRIGATION SYSTEM

Listed below are the steps for repairing water leaks in the irrigation system.

Finding out what caused the publication is the first order of business

It's one thing to locate the leak in your sprinkler system. Finding the precise source is yet another. A leaky pipe, fitting, or valve may be to blame. Before you can fix the problem with the leak, you need to find out where the water is escaping through in the first instance. You might be able to find the leakage source before digging if it is in a valve box. Examine by carefully removing the valve box cover. You might be able to fix the leak without having to dig up if it is coming from a valve inside of a valve box. If a valve box is not leaking, then you will have to dig the area to find the source of the leak.

The leak should be fixed

Once you've determined what caused the leak, you should be prepared to carry out repairs.

PVC Pipes

If you've found that a broken PVC pipe is the source of the leak, it will be necessary to cut off the damaged area to fix it. You can avoid repairing it with a telescopic slip fix if it's a straight section of pipe without any fittings. There is no flexibility with PVC, and therefore in case of multiple fittings, you will have to rebuild it using the same method as when it was first assembled. Make a template out of the cut-out broken part. To accomplish your repair, we advise using purple primer and a high-quality adhesive. If you've never worked with PVC before, PVC pipe repairs might be challenging. After gluing the PVC sections together, give the adhesive at least 20 minutes of cure time.

Swing Pipe/Funny Pipe

The sprinkler head's swing pipe could be the culprit if you discover that a flexible black tube is what's causing the leak. With a barb fitting, these are easily repairable. Simply remove the damaged area, fix it with barb coupler fittings, and use an additional swing pipe.

Sprinkler Head

You might need to replace or repair the sprinkler head if you discover that it was the source of the leak. Replacing the sprinkler head won't solve the issue if the leak continues even after turning off the system. The zone's electric valve needs to be discovered, repaired, or replaced.

Electric Valve

A valve has to be fixed or changed if water is dripping from its side or from multiple sprinkler heads on a zone.

Examine the repair

You must test your repair to ensure it is not leaking before covering it up. To do this, turn on the water supply. Once the sprinkler system stops leaking and your repair is complete, you can cover up your repairs.

 ## 2.8 IDENTIFYING AND LOCATING WATER LEAKS IN THE WASHING MACHINE SYSTEM

There are several distinct reasons why there can be leaks in the washing machine. These leaks are typically caused by aging or defective hardware. There are two types of washing machines. One uses the top load water technology, and the other uses the front load washing technology. You can have several types of leaks based on the type of washing machine that you are using.

Top Load Washer Leaks

The overflow tube may be clogged or slanted if there is a leak in the front. Too much detergent is frequently the source of clogs in the overflow tube. Less detergent is used when doing laundry if the household has soft water or employs a water softener.

Front Load Washer Leaks

If there is a leak under the washer, it may be a sign that the outer drum's seams need to be replaced. If the seam is actually dripping, look for dirt or soap residue there, as well as clean it more frequently. A clogged drainpipe or an improperly attached drain hose are the most frequent causes of a leak in the back for both top-loading and front-loading washers.

Faulty supply hoses

The machine should be emptied and moved away from the wall to check for hose leaks. When the filling cycle starts, check for leaks near the hoses. Hoses are easily replaceable, but if the hose is in fine shape, the hardware that needs to be replaced may be the washers.

Faulty internal hoses

Open the cabinet and look inside for leaks if the washer isn't dripping anywhere from the outside. It is necessary to replace the internal hoses if they are spilling water.

Faulty Pump

If the machine has begun to leak due to the pully sealant, then you are required to replace the pump that drives it. If the belt is significantly damaged or scorched, it could also need to be replaced. The pump can be replaced at home, but if you are not skilled to carry out the job, you should hire a professional.

Broken tub fittings

The only leak that is more challenging to fix than one requiring a new washing machine is one from a bad tub fitting. The specifics of these fixes vary by brand and model. The best course of action if the washing machine is dripping from the tub fittings, is to check the online manual for quick assistance.

2.9 REPAIRING WATER LEAKS IN THE WASHING MACHINE SYSTEM

A washing machine leak causes a lot of trouble since it wastes water, leaves your clothing unclean, and is difficult to clean and dry. Try the following solutions to address typical easy problems that cause washing machine leaks.

The hose clamp can be tightened or replaced

Where the drainage pipe meets the drain hose of your washing machine, there ought to be a connection clamp. Ensure that the clamp is in the proper position; if it's missing or loose, it could lead to a washer leak.

Another option is to change the tub seal

The problem could lie with the tub seal if the water leaks during the rinse cycle. Ask a professional for assistance if you have to disassemble the washing machine and turn it over.

The filter has to be meticulously cleaned

The filter, sometimes known as the catch basket, has the role of clearing the washing machine of any debris. Typically, it is near the drum's edge. The drain hose's end might additionally have a screen that can be removed.

Make sure your washer is leveled properly

Your washing machine may vibrate excessively whilst agitating your clothing if it is imbalanced, which could lead to water spilling out to the floor. To check if the washing machine is balanced, a level should be placed on its top. If not, adjust the washer's feet, or if it has no feet and is an older model, consider buying pads that hinder vibration.

Consider getting a new coupler

The coupler serves as a seal between the motor and the washing machine's drum. The coupler may be broken if the washer won't drain, your clothing is still sopping wet when the cycle is finished, or the appliance is dripping water from the bottom. Its design makes it susceptible to damage if the washing machine stops functioning properly, and it is typically easy to replace.

If the water pump malfunctions, it can be replaced

A malfunctioning water pump frequently results in leaks under washing machines. By looking for moisture in the region below the pump, you can determine if the issue is with the water pump. Look for moisture in this region as well, and make sure the pump hose is connected properly. The issue could potentially be a line that is leaking or a loose hose clamp close to the pump.

2.10 IDENTIFYING AND LOCATING WATER LEAKS IN THE BATHTUB SYSTEM

There are primarily two places where leakage can take place in a bathtub. These are the underlying pipes or the faucet leaks. The grout, tub body, and drain are other places to keep an eye on. There are several repair solutions available to you, depending on the type of leak. However, both kinds of leaks exhibit the same warning indications of problems. Watch out for loose or curling tiles or vinyl flooring, peeling or flaking paint, old wood finishes, ceiling stains from water, mold on the wall or floor, and general pooling around the tub's base. Early detection of these warning signals may be the key to preventing more serious problems in your bathroom. The leak can only be fixed after it has been located. If you can see water dripping from any place, then it can help you determine whether there is a leakage in the grout or faucet. Wipe the exterior of the tub until it is fully dry. Then it should be lined with newspapers to check for leaks. Keep watching closely. The tub should be filled to the edge with water. This helps you in performing the draining test. You are responsible for ensuring that the hole in the roof has been patched. In the event that this is not the case, it is probable that it indicates an issue with the outflow that is blocked. Moreover, the water shall also start to drain. If none of the aforementioned problems are present, your pipes are to blame.

2.11 REPAIRING WATER LEAKS IN THE BATHTUB SYSTEM

Here is how you can repair water leaks in the bathtub system.

Faucet

When you turn off the supply of water completely, then you can initiate the procedure for repairing the faucet. Plastic caps should be removed from the faucet's center. After that, you will be able to remove the spout from the faucet. You can accomplish this with the help of a hammer. To take off the packaging nut, you need to make use of a tool.. Newly installed fixtures should be secured subsequent to the stem washers' replacement. In the end, the supply of water can be restored.

Tub

You're going to need a strong sealant with waterproof properties if you want to fix leaks in the actual bathtub. Dry the area, then liberally coat the cracks with sealant. To smooth the sealant on the tub's surface, use sandpaper.

Drain

There is a possibility of an issue with the putty. This happens when the tub water drains with force. Remove the drain plug and apply putty to the affected area. Screwdrivers can be used for the said task. You can buy this from any good shop.

2.12 DEFECTS IN THE UNDERFLOOR HEATED SYSTEM: HOW TO DETECT AND REPAIR THEM

If you currently possess an underground heating arrangement, it is imperative that you are familiar with the signs of trouble that indicate it is not operating at its optimal level. It will be easy to identify a pipe leak if you have the requisite knowledge and skills. The most evident indications that the underfloor heating system has started to leak are as follows:

A floor with wet or damp spots

It's better to check for leaks if you feel any dampness or spot any such area. If the wetness returns, dry the area out and check to be sure that the system has begun to malfunction.

Mildew or mold

Mold or mildew growth may be a sign of persistent wetness brought on by a leaking pipe.

Cracks in the floor

Wood that has been exposed to moisture may swell and develop cracks. As rapidly you begin to find fissures in the carpeting, you should check for moisture.

Inadequate heating

It's possible that the hot water is managing to leak into some areas of your floor if you find that they seem warmer than others.

Water costs that are well over average

There could be something amiss if your water bill unexpectedly sky-rockets.

 2.13 FIXING A WARMING SYSTEM'S LEAKING PIPES

How to fix water leakages in a baseboard warmth system is outlined below. By using a jackhammer to chip away the surrounding concrete, we may first expose the pipe so that we can assess the degree of the damage.

First step – Damaged section should be cut off

With a PEX cutter, we'll start by removing the damaged portion. In order to remove all of the damage, we will cut the shortest possible section of pipe.

Second Step – Prepare the pipe

The pipe reamer should be used for reaming the ends of a pipe to create smooth edges. This enables our fitting to create an excellent seal on the pipe's end. The pipe's end is prepared for fitting by the reamer's smooth edge.

Third Step – Take a new pipe

The next step is the replacement of the pipe's portion that was removed by cutting a new section of the PEX pipe. We might be able to fix the broken area with one small piece if it was only a tiny portion of the structure.

Fourth Step – Fittings should be attached

We put the fittings and olives onto the pipe's end after first pushing the nuts over the pipe's end. The replacement pipe portion that will fit in the middle is treated in the same way. The fittings can then be connected by screwing the nuts on to the bushes.

Fifth Step – Nuts should be tightened

With the use of a plumber's grip and a spanner, we must tighten the nuts.

Sixth Step – Check for leakage

The replacement fitting will then be put through a pressure test to ensure that it is correctly sealed. The underfloor pipes need to be refilled with water at the manifold, and the pressure must be maintained.

Wrapping the repaired fitting with waterproof tape is a good idea. This prevents corrosion by keeping the concrete away from the metal.

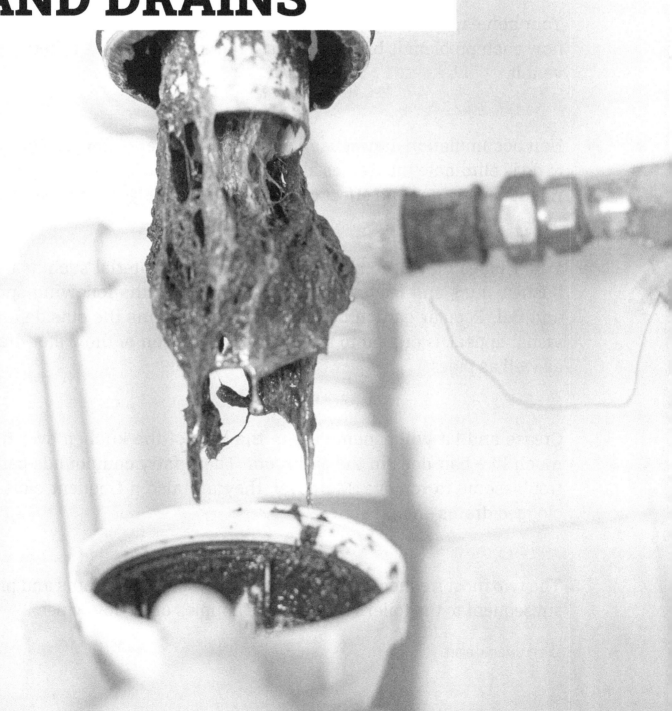

CHAPTER 3
UNCLOGGING AND CLEANING BLOCKED PIPES AND DRAINS

We need to discuss liquid drain cleaners before delving too deeply into the typical reasons for pipe blockages and the various unclogging techniques. Liquid drain cleaners are just for slow drains, whether they are caused by food, hair, or other things. Because of the corrosive qualities of these substances, the blockage is removed, allowing wastewater to pass. They must be handled carefully, and it's a good idea to put on safety goggles, gloves, and a respirator.

 ## 3.1 COMMON CAUSES OF PIPE BLOCKAGES

Your home may have pipe blockages for a variety of reasons. Knowing how each problem is brought about in detail will help us to better prevent it.

Pipe Blockage from Hair

Hair accumulation may cause a pipe to get blocked. Often, all you need to do is eliminate the tresses although if the issue isn't fixed quickly, it might cause a domino effect of complications.

Plants and dirt also block pipes

Water pipes may become clogged by organic material such as trees, bushes, mud, and leaves, especially in the months following spring and fall. Regular garden upkeep, which maintains the outside area's visual appeal, is crucial to the effective operation of the water drains as well as pipes.

Grease accumulation is another factor for a pipe blockage

Grease and fat will accumulate in the sink of the kitchen over time, much like hair does in the bathroom. These fatty compounds can be troublesome to remove. Moreover, they are also a frequent cause of clogged drains and pipelines.

Toiletry-related blockages in pipes

The two most frequent items that cause blockages in drains and pipes subsequent to the toilet's flushing are nappies and baby wipes.

Pipe Blockage from heavy rainfall

There is a significant possibility that a clogged drain has to be unclogged when rainwater overflows from gutters and downpipes.

The pipes are harmed

Water main breaks can be caused by both root damage and normal deterioration. The pipe is more prone to clogs than pipes that are in good condition once they start to fracture.

Pipe clog due to insufficient water flow

Your pipes' water contains dissolved minerals that can accumulate on metal surfaces. As a result, it frequently happens for items like showerheads or portions of taps to get clogged and lower the water pressure.

Pipe blockage because of poor installation

Costly pipe, as well as drain blockages, can be caused by improper pipe installation.

3.2 USING CHEMICAL PRODUCTS AND NATURAL SOLUTIONS TO UNBLOCK PIPES

Listed below are natural solutions and chemical products for unblocking pipes.

Baking Soda + Vinegar

- First, half a cup of baking soda is to be poured down the drainpipe. Then pour half a cup of vinegar.
- The drain should be plugged and allowed to remain in this condition for one hour.
- Then a boiling water pot is to be poured down the drain. The process should be repeated based on the requirement.

Baking Soda + Lemon Juice

- First, half a cup of baking soda is to be poured down the drainpipe.

- The drain should be plugged and allowed to remain in this condition for one hour.
- Then a boiling water pot is to be poured down the drain.

Baking Soda + Salt

- Combine a half container of baking soda to be used with a quarter cup of usual salt. Mix them properly. Then the mixture should be poured down a drainpipe.
- You should wait for half an hour.
- Then a boiling water pot is to be poured down the drain.

Baking Soda + Salt + Cream of Tartar

- You need to mix half a cup of salt, half a cup of baking soda and two tbsp. Of cream of tartar in a sealable.
- Half the quantity of the prepared compound should be poured down the drain. Half the quantity should be saved for future use.
- Then a boiling water pot is to be poured down the drain. Wait for around 60 minutes.
- You can subsequently use tap water to clear the drain.

Salt + Borax + Vinegar

- First, a quarter cup of salt is to be poured down the drainpipe. Then pour a quarter cup of Borax.
- Then half cup of vinegar is to be poured.
- Then a boiling water pot is to be poured down the drain. Wait for around 60 minutes.
- You can subsequently use tap water to clear the drain.

Caustic Soda

Another chemical that can assist with drain cleaning and unclogging the bathroom and kitchen as well as outside drains is caustic soda, sometimes referred to as sodium hydroxide. Caustic soda can be used to clean away waste such as dirt, food, hair, and more.

Sulfuric Acid

While sulfuric acid functions in a way identical to caustic soda, the amount utilized depends on how severe the blockage is. A stronger concentration of the acid-containing drain cleaner might be required if pouring boiling water down the drain doesn't work to clear the blockages.

 ## 3.3 REMOVING CLOGS USING DEVICES LIKE SINK AUGMENTATION AND SEWER REPTILES

Listed below are the ways sink augers and drain snakes can be used for removing blockages.

Drain Snake

You must understand how to utilize a drain snake to remove a blockage if you're trying to figure out how to unclog a drain, whether it's a bathroom or kitchen sink drain. A drain snake is typically the next step if you have a large blockage in the drains which a plunger or other DIY solutions can't clear. Due to its ability to penetrate a plumbing system deeply, it is utilized to remove difficult-to-remove blockages that other tools can't truly handle. The snake's metal cable's head should be inserted down the drain until some resistance is felt. Once this occurs, gradually move the handle clockwise while tightening the clamp. Avoid using it too firmly. If you hit a blockage, continue to extend the cable into the drain. Rotate the metal cable to press it into the blockage and dislodge it.

Sink Auger

Use a drain snake if soft blockages located farther down the line are the cause of your sink, shower, or tub drain emptying slowly or not at all. Water drainage issues that cannot be resolved with chemicals, plunging, or a plastic hair snake can frequently be resolved by augering or snaking a drain. The cable of a snake can extend up to twenty-five feet. A corkscrew-shaped spring at the cable's end unclogs drain obstruc-

tions. The cable moves through the drain when manually pushed after uncoiling from the drum. The drum is secured into position, allowing the cable to revolve when the snake cable's corkscrew end comes into contact with the obstructing element. Its pointed end grips the obstruction when it turns, holding onto it until it can be pulled back as well as removed.

3.4 REGULAR CLEANING AND MAINTENANCE OF PIPES TO PREVENT CLOGS

Since drains plus pipes are solely intended to carry water as well as human waste, they struggle when additional items or materials enter the system. F.O.G. is one of the major dangers to drains as well as pipes, particularly in the kitchen. Instead, collect and keep your F.O.G. in items such as spare mason jars so you can get rid of them properly afterward. Using a drain cover with a strainer will also give additional protection for your pipes, but make sure you clean it off every day. Common items that can clog your drain are:

- Egg Shells
- Paper Towels and Non-Flushable Paper Products
- Pasta and Rice
- Cat Litter
- Fat, Oil, and Grease (F.O.G.)
- Coffee Grounds
- Flushable Wipes

The drains should be flushed with hot water

Regularly cleansing your pipes with hot water is another simple technique to maintain the pipes and avoid a clog. Water that has been heated to a boiling point and then poured down the drain will aid in the breakdown of materials that have accumulated in your pipes, enabling full flow.

The drains need to be cleaned frequently

Without using any tools, you can keep the pipes clear if you maintain and clean them on a weekly basis. Simple solutions like warm water, white vinegar, and baking soda can help your pipes function properly. You could end up saving a lot of money and stay away from worries by completing this little activity.

Consider spending money on yearly drain cleaning services as well

If you are willing to spend money by hiring the services of a plumbing company, then you can ensure the perfect functioning of your plumbing system. You can only accomplish so much without the equipment, expertise, and training. By spending money on annual drain cleaning services, you can ensure that your pipes are free of blockages throughout the year and lower your risk of blockage or pipe damage.

Thank you from the bottom of my heart
for choosing to read this book!

It is with immense gratitude that I address these words to you. It gives me enormous pleasure to know that you have decided to give your time and attention to these pages that I have written with commitment and dedication.

Creating this book has been an exciting journey, and my hope is that you have found it as enjoyable and inspiring to read as I have in writing it. Every word was carefully chosen with the goal of conveying a message, a story or a new perspective to you.

I am aware that you have a multitude of choices available to you when it comes to books, and the fact that you chose mine is a source of great pride and happiness. Your choice is invaluable to me, as it is the support and interest of readers like you that give meaning to my work as a writer.

If you have enjoyed the journey you have taken with these pages, I kindly ask you to **share your experience with others**. Reader reviews are a vital tool for raising awareness of a book and helping other readers make an informed choice.

If you feel inspired to do so, you might **take a few minutes to write a positive review** in which you could share your opinions. Even a few words can make a huge difference and help introduce the book to a wider audience.

CHAPTER 4
TOILET
TROUBLESHOOTING

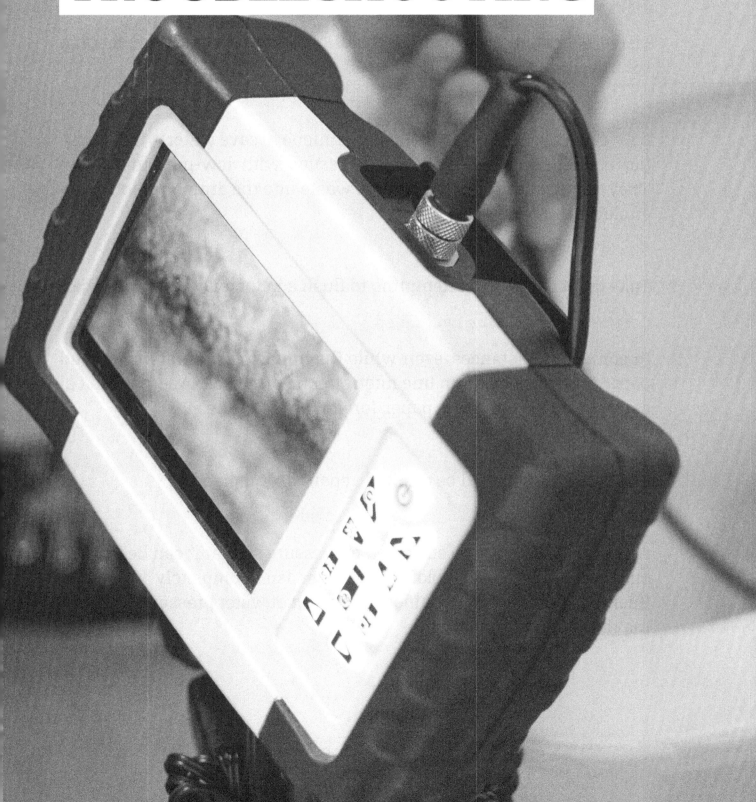

Toilet issues like a toilet that fills slowly, runs, leaks, is noisy, or is clogged might not need a plumber. For many issues, there are simple do-it-yourself (DIY) solutions. Problems like a leaky toilet base and a non-flushing toilet are simple to identify and fix.

4.1 CLOGGED TOILETS - CAUSES AND SOLUTIONS

Listed below are the main causes of clogged toilets and unclogging solutions.

Cause-The Low-Flow Toilet Isn't Powerful Enough

Low-flush toilets are an excellent technique to save water while flushing the toilet; however, they have issues with low-pressure water. They are unable to effectively force waste into the drains, which causes clogged toilets.

SOLUTION

Take great care when attempting to flush a lot of toilet paper at once.

Cause-The Drain Line is Clogged

In some circumstances, even while flushing only ordinary trash and paper products, the drain line might frequently block. Another typical cause of clogged toilets is paper, foreign objects, hair, etc.

SOLUTION

The drain lines should be cleaned, repaired, or replaced.

Cause: The tank doesn't have enough water

Any excrement must be subjected to pressure so that it can be flushed out of the toilet. If the holding container isn't completely full before flushing, there won't be a sufficient amount of water pressure for flushing the waste from the dish.

SOLUTION

Before checking the water line supply for leaks, confirm that the supply valve is not in the closed position. Replace the fill valve if this is not the issue.

Cause- Hard Water Build-Up

The space that both waste and water can pass through can get smaller in toilets with hard water because it might calcify and create a white substance that is challenging to remove. The minerals that build up in the plumbing due to hard water may increase the likelihood of toilet clogs.

SOLUTION

To clean out your toilet system, you could use a solution. Installing a water softener to cleanse the water prior to its entry into the toilet is a long-term treatment that helps prevent future issues with your toilet by minimizing mineral buildup.

Cause- Clogged S-Trap

Sewer gases shouldn't enter your home through the toilet drain, thanks to S traps. It is located behind the toilet. Although helpful in this sense, they could clog easily.

SOLUTION

By utilizing the proper instrument, you can remove a small obstruction from the drainpipe.

Cause-Flushing "Flushable" Wipes

Baby wipes are the main culprit behind clogged toilets, as well, as they can cost you a lot of money in plumbing repair.

SOLUTION

Particularly if you use a septic system, never flush any claimed "flushable" wipes. To avoid clogged toilets, dispose of them in the garbage instead.

Causing-Flushing Foreign Objects

The next frequent reason for clogs is kids flushing toys along with other objects down the toilet.

SOLUTION

Never flush garbage or any other items down the toilet. Children should be watched closely and told to keep toys as well as trash out of the bathroom.

Cause- Clogging because of the flush handle or flapper

A blockage or issue with the lift chain, flapper, flush handle, flapper, or water level could cause a clogged or slowly flushing toilet.

SOLUTION

Inspect the flush handle and perform any necessary adjustments if it's too tight or too loose if the toilet won't flush. Then, after inspecting it, replace or adjust the flush lever lift arm. Make sure the lift chain is securely fastened to the lift arm as well as the flapper at the bottom of the flush valve. As necessary, untangle or adjust. The flapper must completely seal the opening of the flush valve. Replace the flapper if it has been broken or is bent.

 ## 4.2 REPAIRING OR REPLACING THE FLUSH TANK

It is a daunting task to fix a leaky toilet tank. The initial move is to determine what caused the leak. After that, you can continue mending the toilet tank.

Disconnect off the drinking water input to the lavatory and investigate the source of the leak

Find the shutoff valve, which is attached to the pipe behind the toilet. To stop the flow of water, turn this valve as far counterclockwise as you can.

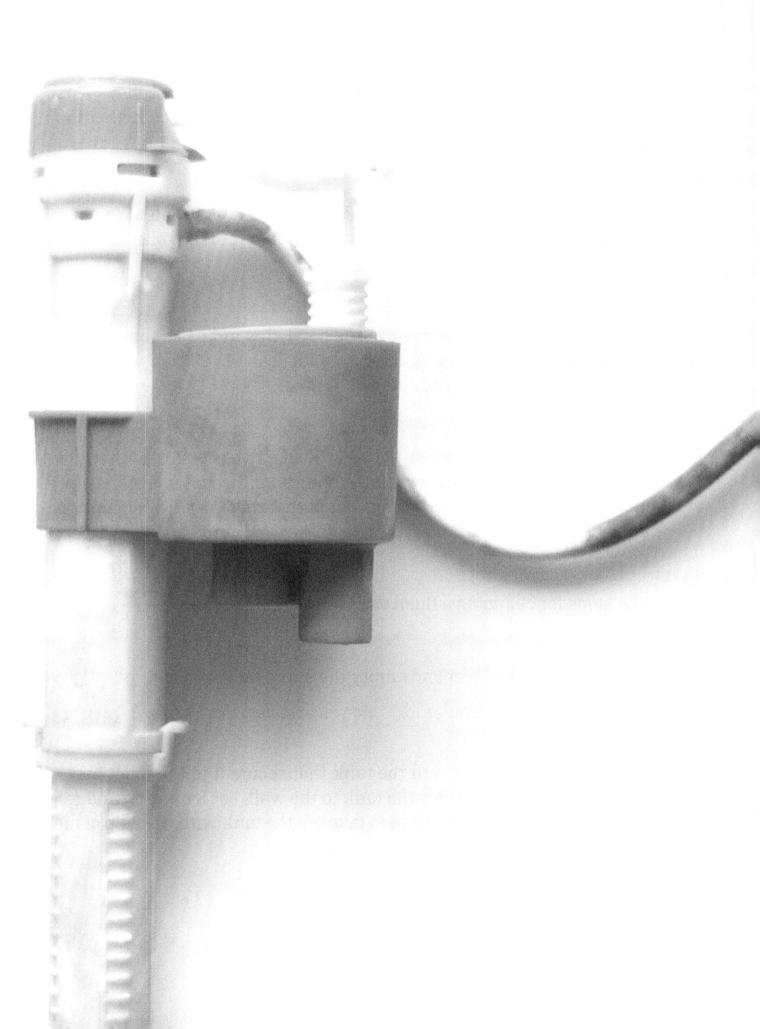

Tank's water level should be marked with the help of a marker

Make the mark where the water in the tank's rear reaches. This should be the highest point. You can use this to ascertain whether the tank's water level rises or decreases over time.

Put food dye into the water

Ten drops of food dye should be added to the tank's water. You can check to see if water from the tank is dripping into the toilet bowl by coloring the water this way.

Check to determine if the liquid's hue has shifted

If there is any sign of the color in the bowl, this indicates that a damaged flush valve is what is causing your leak. The flush valve will need to be replaced if it is damaged.

Check if the tank's water level has risen or decreased

If the water level has decreased, your flush valve is leaking. Check to see if there is water in the overflow tube and if the water level has increased. Additionally, this can be a sign that there is a leakage in the fill valve, which in turn is spilling water into the tank.

Know how to replace a Flush Valve

The steps for changing a flush valve are as follows.

Start by turning off the toilet's water supply

This will flush the toilet and empty the entire tank of water.

The nuts holding the toilet tank as well as the supply tubes in place must now be removed

There are two bolts beneath the tank that secure it to the toilet bowl, and the supply tube fastens the tank to the wall. For loosening and removing the said nuts, you have to take out the tank with the help of an adjustable wrench.

The tank should be lifted off the bowl after the loosening of the nuts

The tank should be placed on top of towels to prevent water from spilling onto the floor.

Locknut on the tank's bottom should be unscrewed, and the valve be removed

This is the sizable nut that secures the flush valve in the tank's center. Once the locknut has been removed, the flush valve should be pushed to release it.

It's time for an updated toilet overflow handle

Pull the freshly installed flush button down into the tank entrance to secure it in place. In order to ensure the appropriate installation of the replacement valve, adhere to the manufacturer's instructions.

Locknuts should be tightened using a monkey wrench

Any disconnected components of the flush valve should be reattached. Ensure replacing the gasket covering the locknut.

The tank should be put on the toilet

The nuts holding the tank to the supply tube should be tightened. Then the tank can be filled. Flush the tank when the installation is finished to make sure the leak is completely fixed.

 ## 4.3 REPAIRING THE TOILET FLUSHING MECHANISM

You should look for a damaged flush handle on the toilet. While flushing the toilet, a handle is pulled. This handle is on the cistern's external side. By pressing this handle, you succeed in activating the mechanism for flushing. A broken flush handle or any defect in the same has to be identified so that you can fix it. When the handle is either too tight or loose, it prevents the link from engaging with the flushing mechanism. What you should do is firmly secure the handle's mounting nut. Limescale could make it difficult to operate the handle properly. You just need to clean it properly to make it fully functional. The handle will need replacement if it is damaged.

 ## 4.4 FIXING TOILET LEAKS

Binding bathroom facilities to the surface while tightening the closet fasteners may fix under-toilet water leakage. Slotted screwdrivers or putty knives unscrew bolt nuts. Wrench-tighten bolts individually at the same time. Thrust could split the toilet bottom. It's possible that the leak is going to stop. Removal of the toilet and replacement of the wax gasket may become essential if tightening the bolts does not address the leakage issue.

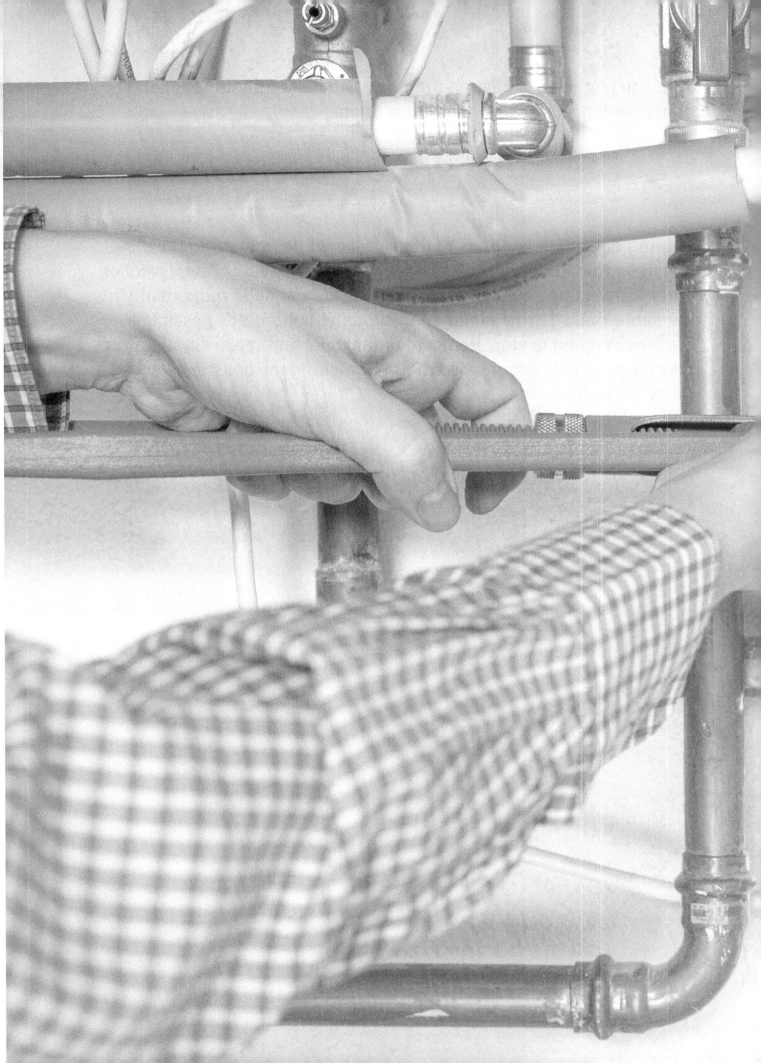

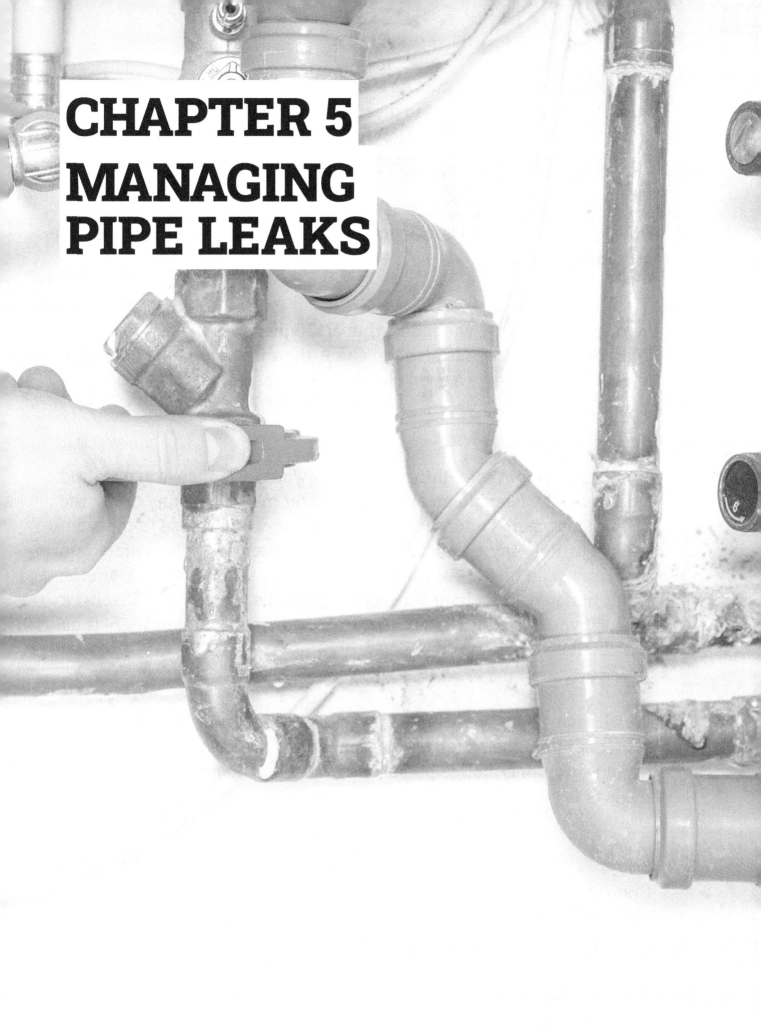

CHAPTER 5
MANAGING PIPE LEAKS

The pipes in your home may be leaking for a variety of reasons, and it's important for homeowners to recognize the damage which a leak may cause by not addressing it. Now we will discuss how to detect pike leaks and repair various types of pipe leaks.

Detecting Leaks in Pipes

Now we will teach you how to detect pipe leaks inside your home and on your property.

The water bill should be monitored on a monthly basis

If you start to receive water bills that are higher than the previous ones and your water usage is also the same, then there must be a leakage issue. Water bills give a good clue to any water leakage.

The water meter should be observed for any unexpected fluctuations as well

If you suspect that something is amiss in your residence, you may find out for sure by keeping an eye on the water meter. In many cases, the meter is concealed underneath a maintenance hole close to the sidewalk. Turn off any circulating appliances, such as dishwashers and close any open hoses. Take a detailed record of the readings from the water metered. In an hour, when you finish the process, double-check again. If you find a fluctuation in the assessments, it means there is an obstruction anywhere.

Look for green spots

We all love greenery. However, if there is a section in the garden that is greener than the rest of the garden, then it is a clear signal of water leakage. You may notice patches of water on the ground's surface if the leak is severe.

It is necessary to perform inspections on both the fittings and the gadgets

Upon identification of water leakage within your house, ensure that the cabinets beneath the kitchen sink are not wet. You should also check for water near the dishwasher, water heater, and clothes dryer, as well as around the bases of the other fixtures in your home. The supply of water should be turned off upon noticing wet spots. You can decide to seek the assistance of a plumbing professional in order to detect and resolve the problem.

Apply the Dye Test to the Toilet

Leakage issues are particularly identified in the house's toilets. Over time, the toilet's flapper may deteriorate and become brittle, enabling water to seep into the bowl from the tank. Food color should be taken, and it should be added to the home's toilet tanks. In case of leakage, you will observe the color of the bowl of the toilet.

Always be on the lookout for Sprawling Clues

Keep an eye on the following to prevent further leakage issues. This will help you in warding off any future hassles with regard to the leakage:

- A discolored wall can be the result of water leaking beneath the drywall.
- Paint or wallpaper that is bubbling or bulging indicates that the wallboard is damp.
- Sometimes leaks can be heard, which might help you detect them.
- In certain instances, you might see black spots on the wall's exterior, but mold frequently grows on the wall's inside where you can't see it. A weird and unpleasant smell gives a clue about the leakage.

Repairing Visible Pipe Leaks

Try one of these methods to fix visible pipe leaks.

Use a Fiberglass Tape

Before putting the leak tape, be sure to wipe the damaged portion of the pipe with a wet cloth. Then, the water should be turned on after waiting for fifteen minutes. As a result, the glue has a chance to set and seal, completely stopping the leak.

Spray for pipe repair

For short-term leak repairs in guttering, pipes, drains, windows, and roofs, a pipe repair spray is appropriate. As it seeps into the holes and cracks, it seals the holes.

Use Epoxy Putty

Using epoxy putty on the broken pipe is another quick and simple plumbing leak fix technique. The epoxy putty will seal a small leak in a pipe after being applied as a result of hardening into a solid surface.

Employ a repair sleeve

A clamp and rubber gasket patch make up a pipe repair sleeve, which is used to firmly seal a broken pipe section.

Use a Slip Coupling

A slip coupling can also be mounted on your pipe. Slip couplings join two pieces of pipe in a watertight manner. Make sure it is the same diameter and size as your current pipe and is made of the same material, such as PVC, copper, etc. before you buy one.

5.1 REPAIRING LEAKS IN PIPES WITHIN WALLS OR FLOORING

Let us learn how to repair leaks in pipes within walls or flooring.

Leaks within flooring

To repair the broken pipe, use epoxy pipe liners. A camera check will be performed to determine the degree of the damage. After cleaning the pipe and inserting the epoxy pipe liner, inflating it, and leaving it to cure. It's possible to complete the entire process in a short amount of time.

Leaks within the walls

Following are the steps for fixing the leaks within the walls.

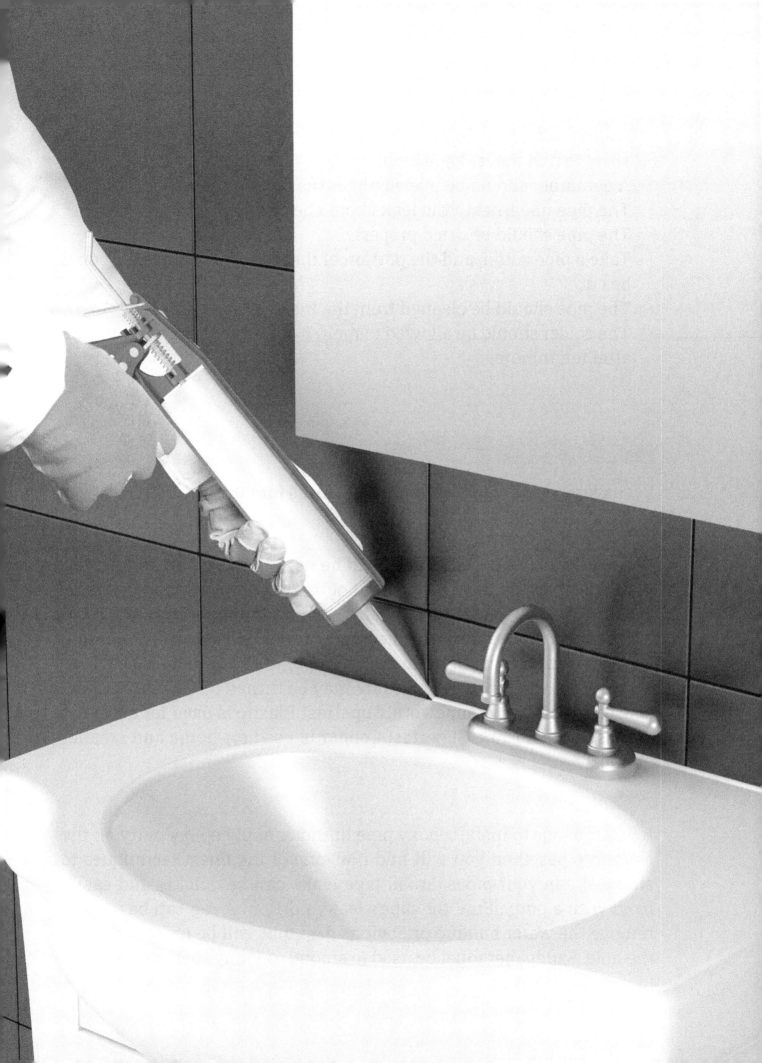

- After ascertaining the location of damage, the wall should be cut for easy access.
- Failing to find the location of damage can force you to use a cloth sheet to find the leakage point.
- A container should be placed under the broken pipe.
- The pipe underneath the leak should be cut.
- The pipe should be dried properly.
- Take a pipe cutter, and the portion of the pipe above the leak should be cut.
- The pipe should be cleaned from the inside and outside.
- The solder should be allowed to melt. It comes to room temperature after ten minutes.

 ## 5.2 USING SEALANTS AND RESINS FOR PIPE LEAKS

Let us learn how to use sealants and resins for pipe leaks.

Sealants

Wrap & Seal Pipe Burst Tape should be used to fix live leaks in situations when the water pressure cannot be shut off. Self-fusing silicone is used to make Wrap & Seal. When stretched through the tube, it combines and creates a firm flexible band about the leaky site, providing an intervention that can withstand temperatures of up to 200 °C. Use epoxy putty whenever the pressure may be turned off. Superfast Steel is used for industrial pipework, Superfast Plastic is used for all forms of plastic tubing, and Superfast Copper is used for home and smaller piping.

Resins

If you manage to install epoxy pipe lining or apply epoxy putty on the leaking pipes, then you will find it as one of the finest techniques to stop leaks in your pipes. Small pipe leaks can be quickly and easily fixed with a putty. Find the pipe's leaky portion. A rag can be used to remove the water buildup or obvious drip that will be present around the hole. Sandpaper must be used to smooth out any rust or damage to the pipe in order to clean it and get it ready for the epoxy putty. Typically, epoxy putty is sold in two separate components. These are a hardener and resins. The adhesive, as well as hardening ingredients, must be mixed together to produce a chemical reaction. Given that the epoxy will solidify in a brief period of time, quickly combine the putty as well as press it against the damaged section of the pipe.

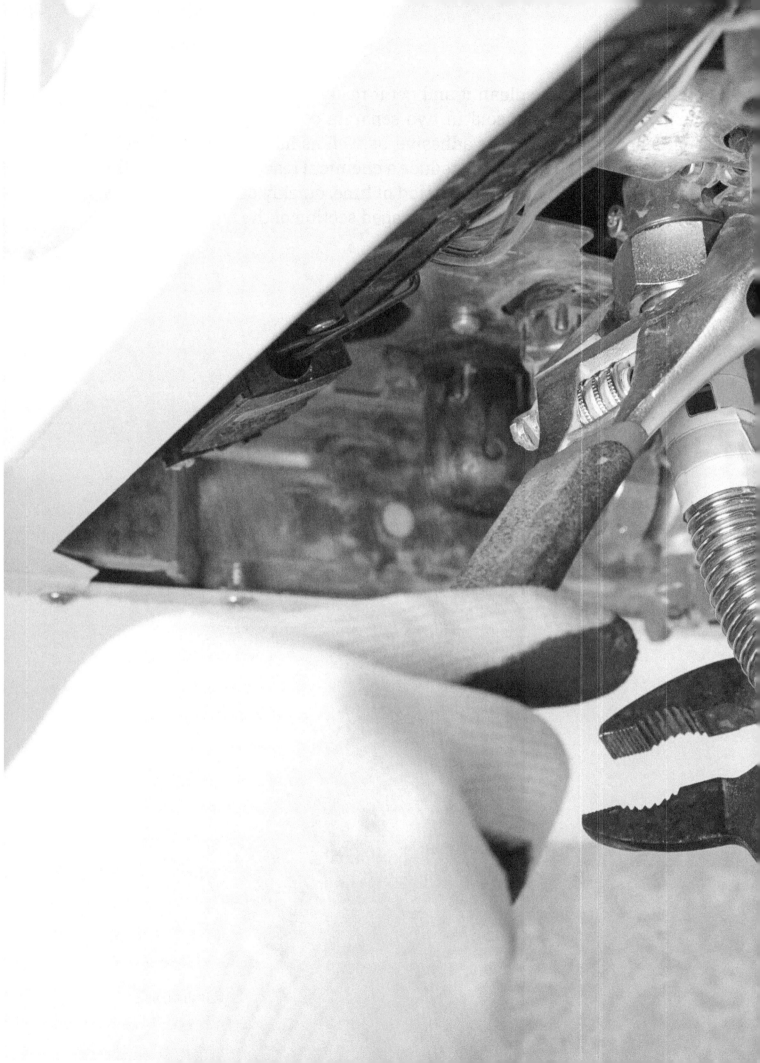

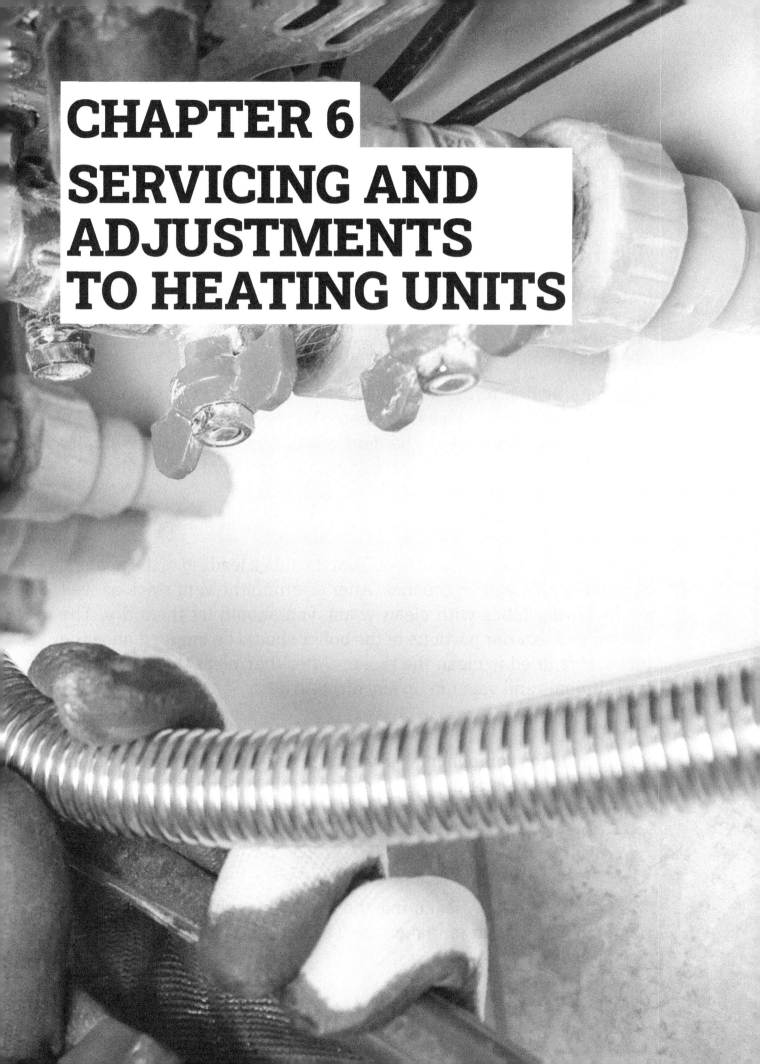

CHAPTER 6
SERVICING AND ADJUSTMENTS TO HEATING UNITS

Your furnace and system can be safeguarded by performing routine home heating system maintenance. With diligence and knowledge, you can keep the heating equipment running smoothly and efficiently. To handle minor things, you don't have to be an expert.

6.1 BOILER MAINTENANCE AND CLEANING

Listed below are the steps required for boiler maintenance and cleaning.

The boiler should be turned off

The main switch to the boiler should be found and then turned off. Patiently waiting for at least two hours has been suggested to prevent burns. During this period, the device will cool down. Screwdrivers should be used for removing the front, top, and vent stack when the boiler has cooled off.

Tubes should be scrubbed, as well as Boiler Unit should be cleaned

To remove carbon, dust, and soot from the tubes leading to the heater's base, use your cleaning brushes. After cleaning the vent stack as well as the burner tubes with clean water, you should let them dry. The bottom and exterior portions of the boiler should be emptied once the tubes have dried to clean the region. After that, clear the area of any impediments and vacuum up any dirt and dust.

The unit should be reassembled and restarted

Reassemble the components as well as restart the system after cleaning the boiler. Wait for the thermostat to reach its regular setting before searching for a blue flame. Afterward, make sure the heating system is operating normally.

Additional advice for maintaining a residential boiler

You should routinely examine the following while cleaning your home's boiler system to make sure it's operating correctly and effectively:

- Flues and air vents should be checked for blockages.
- It is important to keep the water coming from the boiler temperature steady.
- Maintain vigilance in looking for water damage.
- Lime-scale buildup and hard water should be checked and cleaned.
- The boiler should be lubricated properly so it keeps functioning smoothly.
- The boiler chamber must not be permitted to become a dust trap.
- The boiler's water should be flushed to remove dirt as well as grime build-up.

6.2 REPLACING OR REPAIRING RADIATORS

Following are the steps for repairing a radiator.

Nuts should be tightened

Reduce the thermostat's setting, as well as wait for the radiator to cool if water is dripping from beneath the handle. Use groove-joint pliers for tightening the packing nut (near the handle) and a pipe wrench to tighten the bigger Union nut. If that fails to fix the problem, proceed to the next step.

The radiator should be drained

When using a hot water system, the radiator must be drained of water. Turn the temperature regulator down before hooking up a drainage cable to the boiler's drainage mechanism. A valve should be opened for draining the system after running the hose to a floor drain. Open all of the radiator bleeder valves. You should start from the home's top floor.

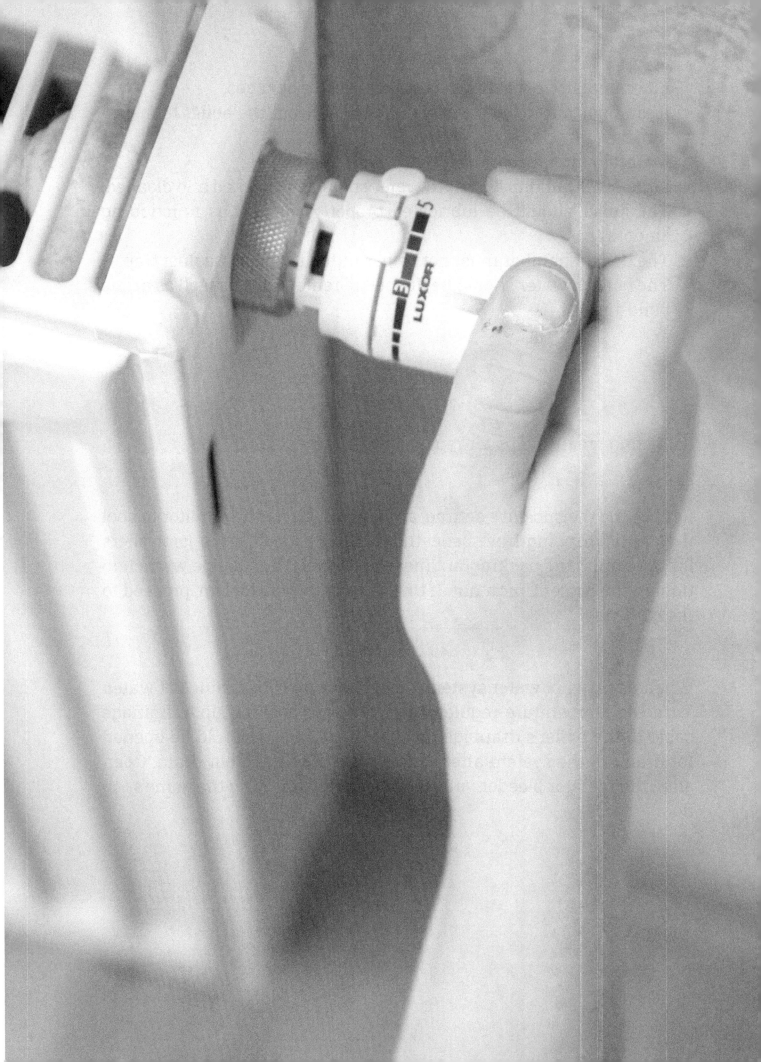

Wrap the Stem

Remove the stem by first unscrewing it and then drawing it out after removing the packing nut. Wrap the stem in strand packing as well as reinstall it if the leak is coming from right under the handle. Continue to the following step if the leak is smaller or if this doesn't fix the issue.

The valve needs to be replaced

To remove the valve from the pipe, first, detach the union nut holding it to the radiator. Find a precise replacement for the old valve; make sure it fits before purchasing. The short pipe coming out of the radiator might also need to be replaced. If required, replace the pipe before installing the replacement valve and union nut.

6.3 REPAIRING LEAKS IN HEATING SYSTEMS

You can repair minor and major leaks in your heating system, as explained below.

For minor leaks

Sentinel Leak Sealer should be applied to the system. The company's guidelines must be strictly adhered to.

For larger leaks

If you want to minimize the damage being caused by larger leaks, then think of applying Sentinel Seal X., It will seal the leak in just 30 minutes. Here's the process for applying it:

- Make sure the piping is clean. To get the best deal possible, oil, grease, dust, rust, and other dirt should be removed.
- If you haven't already, release system pressure.
- Apply liberally on a cloth, then tightly wrap the pipe with the material.
- To stop the other parts from curing within the tube, replace the cap right away.
- To help the sealant cure, spray it with water.
- Restore the water pressure after the curing is complete.

6.4 VENTING HEATING SYSTEMS

A vent key and an old rage are required for venting the heating system. You should always vent the radiators from the home's bottom to the top. The top part of the condenser has a nut attached to it, as can be seen. Once you've located it, use your vent key to tighten the radiator nut. Turn it anti after locking the vent key in place. Once you hear the hissing sound of the air exiting from the radiator, keep twisting the key very slowly. A few water bubbles can also come out during the process. Use the vent key to tighten the radiator's nut once the majority of the air has been expelled via the vent and the water is trickling out of the radiator with fewer bubbles. Wipe away any extra water to prevent it from leaking onto your carpet or flooring. Your radiator's been vented at this point. When you have finished venting your radiator, return to the boiler and check to see if the pressure is perfect.

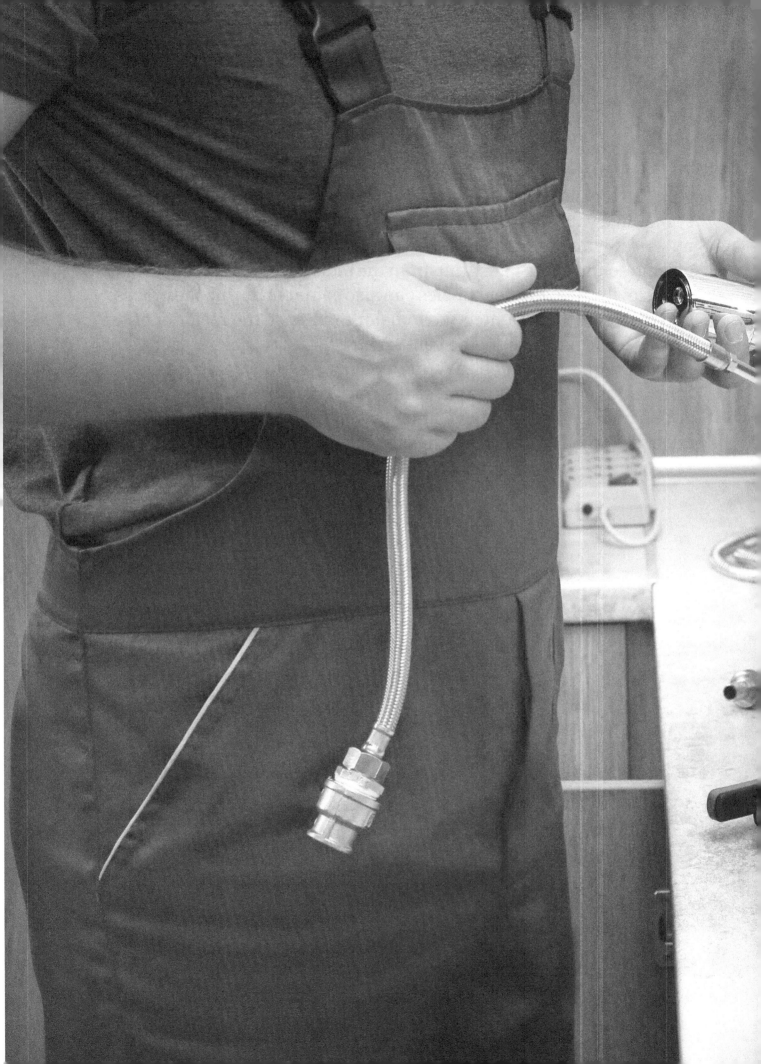

CHAPTER 7
MAINTENANCE OF PLUMBING FIXTURES

It is not unusual for you to counter a plumbing problem in your home. Now we will educate you about plumbing tips so that your plumbing system keeps on functioning smoothly and properly.

 ## 7.1 MAINTENANCE AND CLEANING OF FAUCETS

Listed below are the tips for proper cleaning and maintenance of faucets.

Daily Maintenance

Daily care and maintenance for most faucets is minimal. Most of the time, all you need to do is clean your faucet with a moist cloth as well as a mild cleanser, then dry it with a soft cloth. Window cleaner is also effective on faucets.

Deposits should be cleared and removed

Living in a region with hard water presents additional cleaning difficulties. Frequently, a window cleaner or a gentle abrasive cleaning will work.

Aerator has to be cleaned or changed

Aerators are a crucial component in maintaining faucets. The mineral and dirt buildup that affects a faucet's outside housing also affects aerators. Aerator maintenance is advised once a year, according to experts. All you have to do is take off the aerator from the faucet while maintaining the arrangement of the parts. After that, rinse the components with water and use a toothbrush to scrub the screen.

Perform Other Minor Maintenance

Throughout the life of your faucet, little parts like springs, as well as seats, may need to be replaced due to regular wear and tear.

Thank you from the bottom of my heart for choosing to read this book!

It is with immense gratitude that I address these words to you. It gives me enormous pleasure to know that you have decided to give your time and attention to these pages that I have written with commitment and dedication.

Creating this book has been an exciting journey, and my hope is that you have found it as enjoyable and inspiring to read as I have in writing it. Every word was carefully chosen with the goal of conveying a message, a story or a new perspective to you.

I am aware that you have a multitude of choices available to you when it comes to books, and the fact that you chose mine is a source of great pride and happiness. Your choice is invaluable to me, as it is the support and interest of readers like you that give meaning to my work as a writer.

If you have enjoyed the journey you have taken with these pages, I kindly ask you to **share your experience with others**. Reader reviews are a vital tool for raising awareness of a book and helping other readers make an informed choice.

If you feel inspired to do so, you might **take a few minutes to write a positive review** in which you could share your opinions. Even a few words can make a huge difference and help introduce the book to a wider audience.

7.2 REPAIRING OR REPLACING MIXERS

We have mentioned the actions that you should take when the tap of the mixer is to be repaired:

- The water supply should be turned off.
- Plastic cover should be removed.
- After removing the cap from the mixer handle, you'll discover a grub screw. It can usually be located easily. The base handle is fixed with the mixer tap base with the grub screw. Allen key should be used for undoing the grub screw.
- The retention screw and chromium trim band need to go.
- After gaining access to the cartridge, it should be removed and replaced gently with a new one having the same features and specifications.
- The mixer should be reassembled, and the water supply should be turned on.

 ## 7.3 MAINTENANCE OF WATER FILTRATION SYSTEMS

Follow the steps as mentioned below:

- Avoid using any aggressive cleaning agents and give the system a gentle rinse with warm water.
- Ensure that you regularly clean the system's components, ideally once per week. When cleaning your water filter, be careful to sanitize all of the system's components, especially the water dispenser, line, as well as cap assembly.
- The system should be turned off, a major quantity of salt should be removed, and use hot water to dissolve the obstruction while cleaning your water filter.
- Every time you use your water filter, keep an eye out for visible signs that it might need cleaning. Your water filter frequently also has a monitoring system, which can vary based on the brand or model you have.

- When the filter needs to be changed, the control unit visible on the system of filtration will let you know. This may be shown via a daily status update on the system.
- Keep track of the last time you replaced the filter cartridge, as well as adhere to the recommendations made for that specific cartridge type and your particular system's durability time.

 ## 7.4 REPLACING SHOWER COMPONENTS

Listed below are the steps for replacing shower components.

- It's crucial that the drain should be blocked by placing a drop cloth in the tub or shower.
- The handle or handles must be taken off so that you can easily reach the shower valve.
- Trim Plate should be unscrewed and cleaned. The trim plate can be taken off of the valve stem by first removing the screws and holding it to the valve assembly using a screwdriver.
- Turn off the water.
- The sizes of the shower valve and the current hole in the shower wall should be compared.
- Grab the shower valve stem firmly with a pair of ordinary pliers before gradually removing the cartridge from the shower valve assembly.
- The freshly installed shower valve cartridge should easily fit in once the old one has been removed. Ensure that the shower valve assembly is in good condition. You can use between the latest version or the old ammunition keeper clip to keep the magazine in position.
- Test for leaks after turning on the water.
- Reattach the shower handle and trim plate.

CHAPTER 8
MANAGING LEAKS IN POOLS AND GARDENS

If you do not look after pools and gardens and conduct routine maintenance, then it can lead to a number of problems. Consequently, you will have to face leaking pools and leaking irrigating systems. Pool and irrigation leaks occur if you don't properly maintain or repair damages at the time these are discovered. Now we will explain how to detect and repair pool and garden leaks and repair them.

 ## 8.1 DETECTING AND REPAIRING POOL LEAKS

You will need to take the following steps for detecting and repairing pool leaks. Moreover, you would need a permanent marker, goggles or a snorkel, pool leak detection dye and a syringe.

Equipment should be checked

Check the equipment pad carefully. While keeping an eye out for any evident leaks, switch the pump on and off. You can experience a surprise spray or trickle coming from the apparatus. This might point to a pool system leak, which might also account for the decline in water level.

The pool needs to be inspected

You should move toward the pool inspection if the equipment has no leaks. Don your snorkel or goggles and approach your pool's edges. You should get really close to the edges and floor of the pool to conduct a physical inspection when visibility is excellent.

Search for cracks

Obvious cracks, damage, or anomalies in the pool's structure can be discovered with close observation while you're in it.

Determine the areas which need your focus and attention

Determine which regions are most probable to be the source of the leak by considering the locations of any muddy patches in the yard and any damage to the tiles surrounding your pool.

Pumps or Filtration Systems should be turned off

To locate the source of the breakdown, the pool's drainage level needs to be stable.

Open Leak Detector Dye

If the syringe is empty, add dye while being cautious not to splash any into the pool.

Apply the Dye

Apply the dye to one of the locations you identified in the previous steps. Ensure that the water is still during the entire process.

Observe Closely

You will see the dye leaking through the fracture or crack in the pool if there is a leak. The dye is going to move to and enter the fissure or fracture.

When necessary, repeat.

Apply the dye to additional pool sections where you think there may be leaks as you go. There might be several leak locations, or there might not be any.

Repairing Pool Leaks Easily

The majority of pool leaks are simple to fix once discovered, so you may do it yourself.

- A little amount of pool putty, watertight silicone, a vinyl patch, or a plaster patch is typically used for simple repairs. Pentair Stop Leak can sometimes be used to patch up small plumbing leaks.
- If the leak is caused by a defective gasket, damaged O-rings, or fractured components, you might be able to obtain replacement parts online.
- The most typical pool items required for a leak repair include skimmer gaskets and filter valve components.

- If the leak is caused by a structural crack in the concrete or plaster, you might be able to mend the damage on your own using a little Leslie's Patch-It.

8.2 MAINTENANCE AND REPAIR OF GARDEN IRRIGATION SYSTEMS

Let us now learn how to maintain your garden irrigation system.

Maintenance of Garden Irrigation Systems

The lifespan and effectiveness of irrigation equipment can both be increased with a regular maintenance program. Typically, a preventative maintenance program's foundation consists of the following tasks:

- Daily upkeep includes checking for damp and dry spots, keeping an eye on the pump system, and making sure the central controller is properly programmed.
- A common part of weekly maintenance is checking the operation of sprinklers to make sure they are rotating correctly and to ensure there are no leaks or blocked nozzles.
- Less frequent but significant tasks include raising as well as leveling sprinklers and doing semi-annual pump system maintenance.

Repair of garden irrigation system

You should proceed as follows for repairing the valve.

- The main valve's lid should be unscrewed to expose the rubber diaphragm.
- The rubber diaphragm should be rinsed and dried. This will facilitate the removal of any debris inside.
- The valve should be reassembled, and the irrigation system be tested.

You should proceed as follows for repairing the sprinkler.

- Before re-attaching the filter as well as the sprayer to the sprinkler system, rinse them with clean water to get rid of any obstructions or dirt.
- Remove the soil from around the leaky sprinkler head.
- If the sprinkler's bottom valve is damaged, replace it.
- Check the supply pipe that connects to the sprinkler head for any cracks or ruptures.
- Using a pipe cutter, remove any fractured hose portions and clean the area.
- To ensure a tight connection, the sprinkler valve should be pushed onto the hose.
- To reopen the water supply valve, turn the handle until it is parallel to the pipe. The watering function can be tested by setting the watering method's operator to the default nozzle setting. The sprinkler is fixed if it is spraying properly and there is no water pooling.

8.3 REPAIRING OR REPLACING FOUNTAIN AND SPA COMPONENTS

Your hot tub would need to be drained all the way down to the crack. You need a way of making certain that it is bone dried. After that, two-part epoxy can be used. Take the same quantities of each. Apply the resulting mixture to the fracture. Give it 24 hours to stand.

8.4 PREVENTING WATER LEAKS IN POOLS AND GARDENS

If you don't maintain your pool and garden correctly or fix any damage as soon as it is discovered, leaks will develop. You should address any leaks you notice in your garden or pool immediately. Settlements caused by not doing so could be extensive and costly to fix. You can find a leak before it's too late if you know which regions are prone to it. Whenever each of these problems occur, the water's materials and the filtering system could deteriorate as time passes. The maintenance of the swimming pool's cleanliness, safety, and effective operation depends on these regions, which are essential components of the pool. Pool leaks can be avoided if these locations are properly maintained. By doing periodic upkeep, regular cleanings, and replacing pipes and connections, you can stop a lot of water leaks in your garden. Any faulty pipe connections could also indicate a potential leak down the road. Defects in ponds and landscaping can be avoided with consistent repair and inspection.

CHAPTER 9
HANDLING PLUMBING EMERGENCIES

Plumbing emergencies can put you and your loved ones in challenging and problematic situations. Major leaks can damage your home. They can also be expensive to address.

9.1 PREPARING FOR PLUMBING EMERGENCIES AT HOME

Listed below are the tips for preparing for plumbing emergencies right now.

- Decide on an emergency plumber and store their information on your phone.
- Be able to turn off your water.
- Be on the lookout for plumbing-related hazards, especially those involving electric shock, as well as harmful substances.
- Create a preparation kit in case you are unable to turn off the water valve in your home, or there is already a leak or flood when you uncover the issue.
- To remove sediment, have your water heater tank emptied out after three to six months.
- Avoid clogging sink drains by throwing away oil, grease, coffee grounds, eggshells, and animal bones in the trash instead of in the sink.
- Be familiar with DIY methods and safety precautions.

9.2 IMMEDIATE ACTIONS TO TAKE DURING A PLUMBING EMERGENCY

You should take the following actions during a plumbing emergency.

- Make an emergency plumbing call. To stop further harm, contact a specialist as soon as you can.
- To stop smaller leaks, the water supply at the main should be turned off.

- Moreover, the main water valve can be turned off if there are larger leaks.
- Turning off the water heater will help avoid overheating or other potential problems if you have a serious plumbing emergency.
- Tape the area where a little leak is occurring to stop or reduce it.
- Observe closely and keep records of any leakage so that you may inform your plumber of them when they arrive.
- Remove Clogs & Open Spigots

9.3 CONTACTING AND WORKING WITH PROFESSIONAL PLUMBERS

Some plumbing issues appear to be an easy fix, but the problem never gets fixed. We like performing things on our own whenever we can, but plumbing around bathroom sinks and toilets can be especially risky because leaks may swiftly propagate or go undiscovered in partitions. For instance, the absence of water in pipes might be a huge red flag that something is seriously wrong. As a result, calling a professional plumber is essential. If you experience a drainage difficulty and you're sure you are unable to resolve it yourself, call an accredited plumber in your area. Working with a qualified plumber will help you enhance your DIY skills.

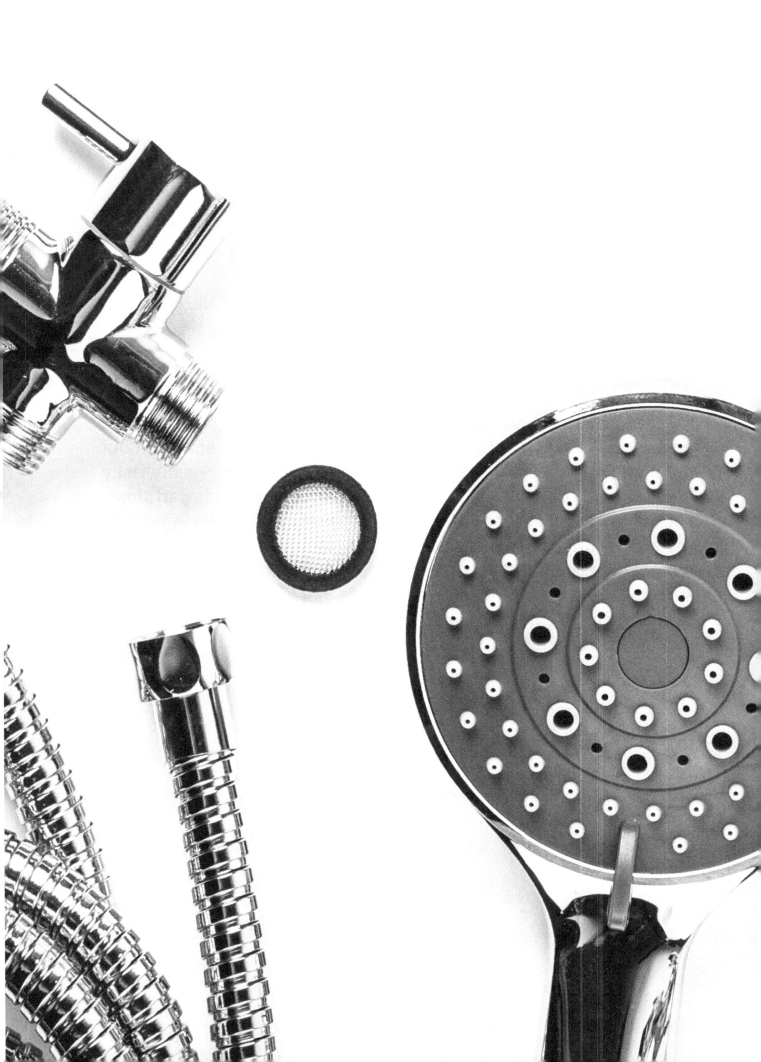

CHAPTER 10 ADVICE ON PREVENTIVE SERVICE

Maintaining a well-running drainage system in the residence requires regular inspection and servicing. It has to be maintained the way you maintain other important things. Without regular upkeep as well as repairs, the plumbing system may eventually begin to malfunction, which could cause serious issues. Finding a cure is always better than prevention, which is typically much less expensive and stressful. The solution is preventative plumbing maintenance, which every homeowner should think about setting up with their plumbing professional.

 ## 10.1 PERIODIC SANITARY REPAIRS AND ITS RELEVANCE

The peace of mind that comes from knowing that the well-maintained plumbing system is functioning properly is what you want to get the most out of preventative plumbing maintenance. Predictive drainage upkeep over the course of several years may conserve a lot of financial resources by avoiding the need for expensive modifications to the drainage system alongside other parts of the home. Periodic plumbing upkeep is not only simpler to do, but also more cost-effective in the long term. Trying to avoid something from happening in the first place is always the better option compared to having to deal with a big problem later.

 ## 10.2 PREVENTIVE MAINTENANCE SCHEDULE FOR PLUMBING SYSTEMS

The plumber visits your house to do a complete and regular inspection of the plumbing system. They will inspect simple stuff like tap washers. Your plumber may examine the plumbing in your home and find that you have outdated pipes that need to be replaced before they start to leak, which can be expensive and dangerous. The greatest common difficulties with drainage in homes are blocked lines. Your plumber can install a CCTV camera down the pipes to look inside of them, even if you aren't presently having an issue with blocked pipes. In this manner, the plumber may assess whether any debris is amassing in the pipes that might eventually cause a clog. A plumber performing preventative maintenance will examine showerheads, fittings under sinks, etc., in addition to the previously stated potential leaky taps.

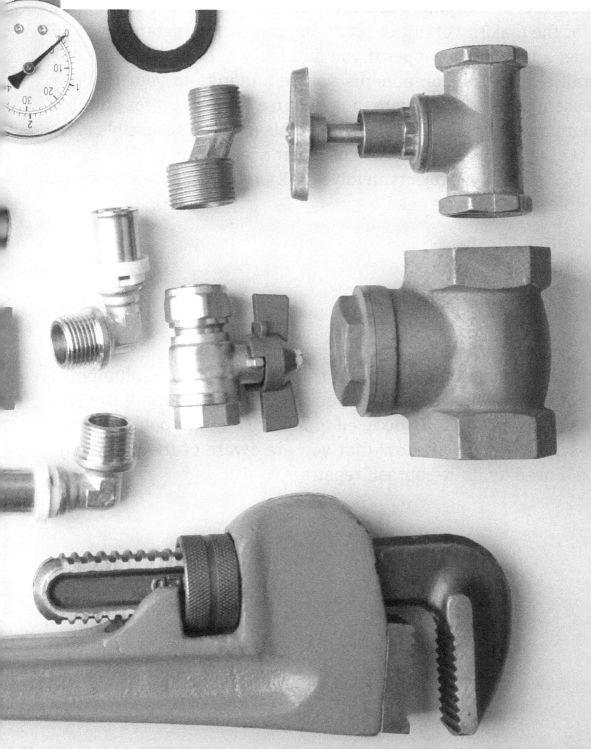

CHAPTER 11
ADDITIONAL RESOURCES AND USEFUL TOOLS

Plumbing tools come in an assortment of varieties, and it's crucial to understand which ones are best suited for certain tasks. You must first comprehend the fundamentals of pipe fittings that are used to connect pipes before making a purchase. You must choose the fittings you'll need before beginning your project.

11.1 TIPS FOR PURCHASING PLUMBING TOOLS

You'll need a set of equipment and instruments called a DIY plumbing tool kit for the majority of minor plumbing issues. For instance, you'll have to get a new toilet flapper if you find out you need one. But you can install a lot of the components yourself, thanks to your toolkit. All the essential instruments are included in a full tool set for plumbers. When you need them, the plumbing tools must be accessible and ready. Let's say you wish to replace or repair a leaky faucet. The most popular DIY plumbing projects involve sink problems. The following are examples of items you need:

• Plastic drain snake
• Sink plunger
• Basin wrench
• Hand auger
• Pliers

For your project, you might also want some particular sink plumbing supplies or components. Make sure you select the appropriate size for your project, for instance, if you need to replace a nut or bolt. You can begin assembling your kit now that you are aware of the plumbing tools you'll need for do-it-yourself repairs.

You can select from our selection of top contractor associations, plumbing blogs, marketing & SEO resources, forums, and other resources.

Industry-Leading Plumbing Blogs

Listed below are the industry's leading plumbing blogs.

- Mr. Rooter Blog
- LettrLabs
- Plumbing Perspective
- Benjamin Franklin Plumbing Expert Tips
- Plumber Mag

Contractor Associations and Resources

The names of contractor groups and other resources are listed below. These organizations can offer you the training as well as networking opportunities you need to be successful. Here are the best sources to consider:

- Nexstar Network Blog
- Service Nation, Inc.
- Len the Plumber

Marketing and SEO Resources

Listed below is the information and data about marketing and SEO resources.

- Plumber & HVAC SEO
- ServiceTitan Blog
- Plumbing Webmasters Blog

Plumbing Forums and Communities

It's crucial to have a group of specialists that can provide guidance and assistance because plumbing is a difficult job. We'll highlight some of the busiest and most useful plumbing forums and forums in this section so you can connect, exchange expertise, and gain from one another.

- Drain Cleaning Forum
- ServiceTitan Masterminds
- The Plumbing Forum
- Reddit Plumbing
- Plumbing Zone

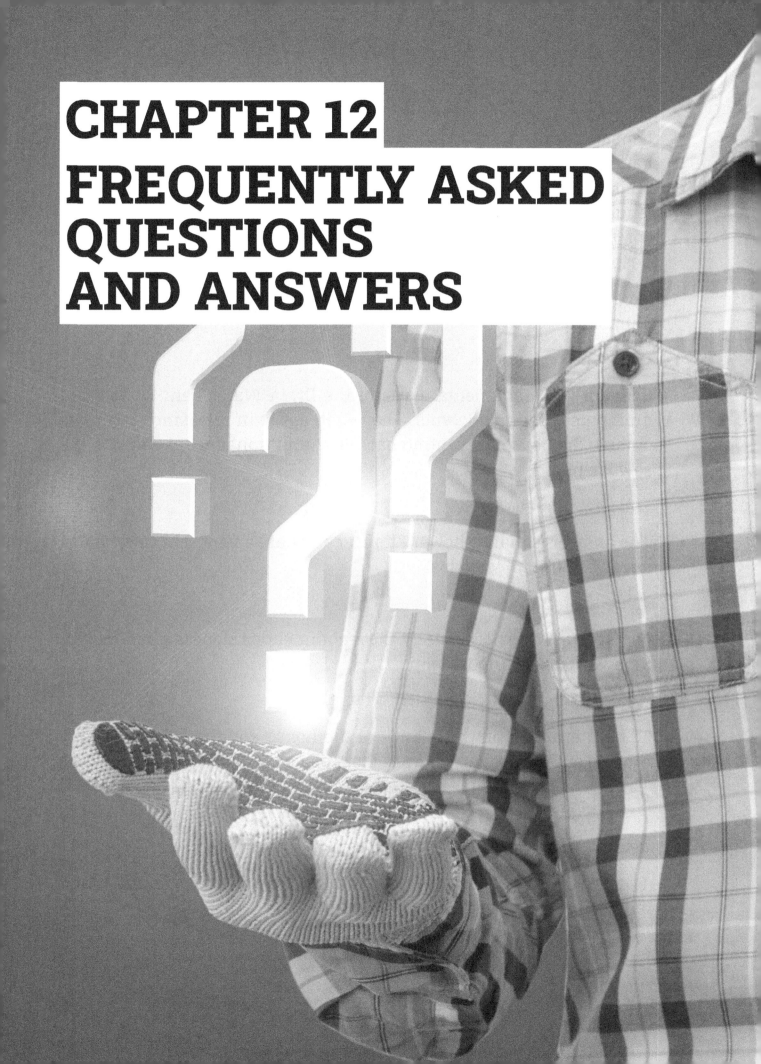

CHAPTER 12
FREQUENTLY ASKED QUESTIONS AND ANSWERS

You do not have to ponder over the home plumbing until something goes wrong, and you have no choice but to address it. Plumbing problems can range in severity from small inconveniences to urgent situations. Overall, it's essential to take a preventative and emergency preparedness approach and to be prepared to face all sorts of challenging situations. As a result, we have compiled this FAQ for your convenience. Home Plumbing: Frequently Asked Problems and Their Responses

Here are the answers to frequent questions about resolving household plumbing issues.

What are some plumbing basics?

Some of the fundamental parts of the Drain Water Vent System are drainpipes, traps, and vents. They each assist in releasing sewer gas outside the house, preventing backflow, and transferring water to the sewage line.

Can a toilet and a shower share a vent?

The answer is that a shower & toilet can share a vent. The toilet must, however, be connected last.

What should the plumbing slope be?

For pipes moving horizontally, the recommended slope is a one-fourth-inch vertical drop/foot of pipe.

Where is the water line located in my home?

The water meter on the outside of the house and the location where the line enters the house are the ideal places to look for the water line. The room, as well as the side of the home where the line enters, should be the same.

To what extent does the cost of fixing a pipe vary?

The cost to repair a damaged pipe can range from $150 to $2,000, based on the length of the line.

Steps required for averting damage that can be caused by water.

You are able to safeguard your dwelling from any kind destruction by taking a few easy precautions. Leakage issues should be identified in the early phase, and your plumbing system should be regularly maintained. As soon as you become aware of the issue, immediately give a trained plumbing a call.

What precautions need to be taken in the event that the tube bursts?

The main valve's water should be turned off the moment you discover the pipe that has been broken. Steps should be taken to save yourself from any hazard.

Can water be drained from the dishwasher?

It can be simple to repair a dishwasher that won't drain. You can check for clogs or attempt to clean the strainer basket.

How can my garbage disposal be fixed?

Whenever the rubbish disposal is malfunctioning in any way, you ought to switch it off and disconnect its connection to the outlet. Next, look inside the cavity for any other obstructions or small objects. Before trying to restart the disposal, make sure the breaker hasn't tripped. Then, reconnect the appliance.

What causes my faucet to leak?

There are several reasons why faucets leak, but the most frequent ones are O-rings, valves, and corroded gaskets.

Why is the cost of my water so high?

Your water bill may increase unexpectedly if there's a leak. Although you are unable to locate the leak at the moment, it may still be there.

Should a tankless hot water heater be installed?

While a certain group is perfectly fine with an outdated hot water heating system, there are a variety of reasons why you might want to consider switching to a disposable hot water heating system. This approach can result in significant financial savings. Additionally, they never use up their supply of freshwater.

Is it possible for me to stop my plumbing from freezing?

On frosty evenings, insulate the pipes well or leave the water on a steady drip.

Which part of my house has the major water consumption?

In a family, the toilet typically uses the most water.

How Can I Prevent Shower and Tub Water Damage?

Avoid the tendency for the water in the shower to pool. Flooding can be used to get around an opening that is damaged. Additionally, promptly dry the floor after taking a shower or a bath. Keep water from collecting on the floor. Dry off the space as much as you can.

Can chemicals be used to clear drains safely?

If you happen to apply caustic solvents to clean drain too frequently, there is a possibility that your drainage system will be damaged. They might contribute to the pipes' degeneration.

How Do I Respond If a Pipe Bursts?

- Do your best to evaluate the incident and the surroundings.
- Turn down the power in any rooms or regions of your property that have been impacted by the problem.
- Take pictures of the damage.

What Should I Do First If the toilet starts to overflow?

- Rush of water should be stopped.
- The plumbing problem's extent and scope should be assessed.
- Unclogging and cleaning the toilet is strongly recommended.

Quick Solutions for Plumbing Emergency Situations

Here are quick solutions for plumbing emergency situations.

What is the quick solution for a toilet-clogged pipe?

Using a plunger is the simplest approach to clear a clogged toilet pipe. The plunger won't operate properly unless there is sufficient water in the bowl to cover its head. If there is not sufficient water, you can add more using a large bowl or similar receptacle.

What is the simple fix for a clogged pipe in a sink?

A plunger may be used to attempt to unclog a clogged drain. Use the plumber's snake once more, if necessary, to quickly empty the pipe.

What is the simple fix for a bath drain blockage?

Hair will be an issue in your bathtub, just like it is in the bathroom sink. Try the same things you'd do with a bathroom sink after removing the drain's cover grate. Hopefully, this will keep your bathroom operating effectively.

CONCLUSION

Most individuals dread fixing their pipes because they lack the necessary information. In such cases, you must depend on a professional plumber to fix plumbing issues even if they can be handled easily with prior knowledge of plumbing systems and tools. If you learn how to plumb, you can also save a significant amount of money by carrying out the repair and replacement yourself.

Everyone wants to be self-sufficient in managing plumbing problems, reduce dependence on professionals, and save money. This can be done by learning and applying the requisite plumbing skills to solve plumbing issues within your home. It's easy to unclog a pipe, open the sink drain, repair water irrigation system pipes, and take measures to prevent future plumbing issues related to clogging, pipe leaks and minor replacements.

This is a must-read book if you want the confidence to address plumbing emergency situations and save your hard-earned money. This book has all the information you require for managing your household plumbing issues. All you need now are the tools to perform the job perfectly and safely. Just refer to the list of tools we included in the beginning of the book. Your toolbox should contain all these tools.

Thank you from the bottom of my heart for choosing to read this book!

It is with immense gratitude that I address these words to you. It gives me enormous pleasure to know that you have decided to give your time and attention to these pages that I have written with commitment and dedication.

Creating this book has been an exciting journey, and my hope is that you have found it as enjoyable and inspiring to read as I have in writing it. Every word was carefully chosen with the goal of conveying a message, a story or a new perspective to you.

I am aware that you have a multitude of choices available to you when it comes to books, and the fact that you chose mine is a source of great pride and happiness. Your choice is invaluable to me, as it is the support and interest of readers like you that give meaning to my work as a writer.

If you have enjoyed the journey you have taken with these pages, I kindly ask you to **share your experience with others**. Reader reviews are a vital tool for raising awareness of a book and helping other readers make an informed choice.

If you feel inspired to do so, you might **take a few minutes to write a positive review** in which you could share your opinions. Even a few words can make a huge difference and help introduce the book to a wider audience.

Made in the USA
Las Vegas, NV
30 October 2023

79939402R00066